Rationing of Medical Care
for the Critically Ill

Brookings Dialogues on Public Policy

The presentations and discussions at Brookings conferences and seminars often deserve wide circulation as contributions to public understanding of issues of national importance. The Brookings Dialogues on Public Policy series is intended to make such statements and commentary available to a broad and general audience, usually in summary form. The series supplements the Institution's research publications by reflecting the contrasting, often lively, and sometimes conflicting views of elected and appointed government officials, other leaders in public and private life, and scholars. In keeping with their origin and purpose, the Dialogues are not subjected to the formal review procedures established for the Institution's research publications. Brookings publishes them in the belief that they are worthy of public consideration but does not assume responsibility for their accuracy or objectivity. And, as in all Brookings publications, the judgments, conclusions, and recommendations presented in the Dialogues should not be ascribed to the trustees, officers, or other staff members of the Brookings Institution.

Rationing of Medical Care for the Critically Ill

Edited by MARTIN A. STROSBERG
I. ALAN FEIN
JAMES D. CARROLL

Report of a conference held in Washington, D.C., on May 27, 1986, sponsored by the Brookings Institution

THE BROOKINGS INSTITUTION / Washington, D.C.

About Brookings

The Brookings Institution is a private nonprofit organization devoted to research, education, and publication in economics, government, foreign policy, and the social sciences generally. Its principal purpose is to bring knowledge to bear on the current and emerging public policy problems facing the American people. In its research, Brookings functions as an independent analyst and critic, committed to publishing its findings for the information of the public. In its conferences and other activities, it serves as a bridge between scholarship and public policy, bringing new knowledge to the attention of decisionmakers and affording scholars a better insight into policy issues. Its activities are carried out through three research programs (Economic Studies, Governmental Studies, Foreign Policy Studies), a Center for Public Policy Education, a Publications Program, and a Social Science Computation Center.

The Institution was incorporated in 1927 to merge the Institute for Government Research, founded in 1916 as the first private organization devoted to public policy issues at the national level; the Institute of Economics, established in 1922 to study economic problems; and the Robert Brookings Graduate School of Economics and Government, organized in 1924 as a pioneering experiment in training for public service. The consolidated institution was named in honor of Robert Somers Brookings (1850–1932), a St. Louis businessman whose leadership shaped the earlier organizations.

Brookings is financed largely by endowment and by the support of philanthropic foundations, corporations, and private individuals. Its funds are devoted to carrying out its own research and educational activities. It also undertakes some unclassified government contract studies, reserving the right to publish its findings.

A Board of Trustees is responsible for general supervision of the Institution, approval of fields of investigation, and safeguarding the independence of the Institution's work. The President is the chief administrative officer, responsible for formulating and coordinating policies, recommending projects, approving publications, and selecting staff.

11-2-89

Editors' Preface

The rapid growth in the cost of providing medical care in the United States is startlingly apparent in the care of critically ill patients. To encourage informed discussion of the issues surrounding intensive care in hospitals, Brookings convened a policy development seminar on May 27, 1986, that brought together health care practitioners, public and private sector officials, and academicians. The panel participants, representing a wide spectrum of interests and viewpoints, exposed many areas of intensive care that are either in dispute or unaddressed. Some of the papers from the conference are gathered here as a contribution to the Brookings Dialogues on Public Policy series. The volume concludes with a set of proposals, developed after the conference, aimed at stimulating further dialogue.

Brookings would like to acknowledge the support of Union College and the Albany Medical College–Ellis Hospital Critical Care Education Foundation, which along with the Brookings Center for Public Policy Education organized the conference and sponsored this publication. The editors wish to acknowledge the valuable conference participation of Jeffrey S. Augenstein, Mary Ann Baily, Howard S. Berliner, J. Richard Gaintner, Dennis M. Greenbaum, James Lambrinos, and Robert M. Veatch. They are grateful to Betsy Cole, Carol Delaney, and Julia Sternberg for their help in organizing the conference and to Alice M. Carroll for editing the manuscript.

Martin A. Strosberg
December 1988　　I. Alan Fein
Washington, D.C.　　James D. Carroll

Contents

Introduction   1
MARTIN A. STROSBERG

Ethics and Scarcity   11
JOHN S. MORRIS

Alternatives to Rationing   17
MAX HARRY WEIL

Lessons from the United Kingdom   24
HENRY J. AARON

Discussion   32

Federal Policy and Intensive Care   37
WILLIS D. GRADISON, JR.

Discussion   41

Criteria for Admission to Intensive Care Units   44
WILLIAM A. KNAUS

Beyond Do-Not-Resuscitate Orders   52
ROBERT BAKER

A Third-Party Perspective on Reimbursement Policy   64
LINDSAY ROBINSON

Triage: An Everyday Occurrence in the Intensive Care Unit   70
DANIEL TERES

Legal Perspectives on the Allocation of Intensive
Care Services   76
BARBARA R. GRUMET

Discussion   80

Professional Ethics and Political Power   82
MICHAEL A. RIE

Caring for the Critically Ill: Proposals for Reform   87
ROBERT BAKER, I. ALAN FEIN,
MARTIN A. STROSBERG & MAX HARRY WEIL

Panel Participants   93

Conference Participants   95

*Rationing of Medical Care
for the Critically Ill*

MARTIN A. STROSBERG

Introduction

The efficient production and distribution of resources has long been a central feature of the debate on a national policy on health care. The issue of rationing, or limiting the use of potentially beneficial resources, has emerged relatively recently.

Nowhere is rationing of greater concern than in the intensive care unit (ICU), the high citadel of technology. In the ICU, highly trained nurses care for critically ill patients using a wide range of life-saving technologies. The vital signs of the patients are constantly monitored. Often there is a ratio of one nurse to one patient for the most severely ill.

A day in an ICU bed is three to four times more expensive than a day in a routine hospital bed. The Office of Technology Assessment estimates that the cost of intensive care for adults (including those in coronary units) represents 14–17 percent of the total inpatient costs in community hospitals, or about $13 billion–$15 billion in 1982. When care in neonatal units is included, the share of total costs rises to 20 percent. In the aggregate, 1 percent of gross national product (GNP) is spent on intensive care.[1]

Many have argued that in terms of increased rates of survival and improved quality of life, investment in ICU services is inefficient. While some patients clearly will benefit from the life-support interventions of the ICU and return to normal life, the chance that many patients in chronically poor health will survive is at best only marginally improved by ICU intervention.

A policy development seminar held on May 27, 1986, at the Brookings Institution, on rationing medical care for the critically ill,

---

1. Robert A. Berenson, *Intensive Care Units (ICUs): Clinical Outcomes, Costs, and Decisionmaking*, OTA-HCS-28, prepared for the Office of Technology Assessment (Government Printing Office, 1984), pp. 4–5.

brought together physicians, administrators, economists, lawyers, politicians, philosophers, ethicists, and third-party payers. One of the two major issues discussed was whether cost containment and efficiency can obviate the need for a policy restricting costly but beneficial life-sustaining care in the ICU. Or will the United States move to a system like Great Britain's where costly but beneficial services are limited at a societal level by centralized governmental budgeting and at the individual level by implicit rationing by physicians? The second major issue, dealing with the allocation of services, asked whether physicians must act as society's gatekeepers in distributing medical services or remain the patient's agent as called for by the Hippocratic Oath. Who, other than the physician and patient, should be brought into the process of deciding whether to limit beneficial services?

In introducing the seminar, John S. Morris traces the cultural forces that have been pushing society to acknowledge the need for rationing and outlines the complex ethical and moral issues that have arisen. He reminds us that scarcity in health services in the United States comes out of abundance, and he questions whether our society can limit its own abuses, legal, social, and cultural.

A CONTINUUM OF PERSPECTIVES

Given that the United States has had very little experience in consciously and explicitly rationing health care, there are naturally differing perspectives on the many questions raised by Dr. Morris.

In casting about for a method to characterize and crystallize the various perspectives, it is useful to use the triage decision as the point of departure. Triage based on medical criteria is one way to make rationing decisions in an equitable fashion. Other criteria, which may or may not be thought to be so equitable, include price, first come–first served, social worth, and age.

Triage is a concept from the battlefield. Where medical personnel and equipment are scarce and time and effort must be put to best advantage, casualties are divided into three groups. The first are those persons not severely wounded who could, probably, get better by themselves or wait for more help to arrive. The second are the very severely wounded, whose recovery is probably hopeless. The third are the in-betweens who would derive the greatest benefit from medical attention. Though there may be some in group one who would benefit from medical attention, and some in group two who could even be saved by spending time and effort on them, many more in group three would not be saved. Nothing is certain. But in terms of saving the greatest number of lives, triage based on probability assessments is a better way of rationing scarce resources than such criteria as first come–first served or treating the most severely ill first.

Initially the perspectives cluster around three points: cutting out only the nonbeneficial medical services, which will result in savings that negate any scarcity and corresponding constraints; cutting out nonbeneficial medical services and, where scarcities like limited numbers of ICU beds or ICU nurses occur, using medical criteria to decide who can benefit most; and cutting out nonbeneficial medical services and marginally beneficial care that is very expensive.

Eliminating the Waste

Max Harry Weil, first president of the Society of Critical Care Medicine, unequivocally rejects scarcity of resources as applicable to the intensive care units. Inappropriate use of resources, yes, but scarci'y of resources, no. The heart of the problem lies in risk benefit analysis. If we could only eliminate those services that bring little or no benefit, there would be enough resources available to provide all beneficial services. Weil cites some obvious examples. It is not rational to treat a 95 percent body burn in a sixty-five-year-old man because no person in such a condition has ever survived. Similarly, in a neonatal unit, no 250-gram infant has survived after birth; treatment makes no sense. This does not mean that experiments under controlled conditions should not be performed to push back the thresholds of failure. But as a routine matter, aggressive treatment for the sake of doing something is irrational and unacceptable. Furthermore, in many cases the risks of infection, psychological trauma, and other complications often outweigh the benefits of intervention. Invasive diagnostic procedures, for example, that provide information that is only marginally useful but are likely to produce iatrogenic illness should be abandoned.

Although, as Weil contends, certain medical procedures are obvious candidates for abandonment, for many others introduced without adequate experimentation there is insufficient information to make a judgment on risks and benefits. To produce that information would require a major investment of scientific resources. Clinical trials are expensive, time consuming, and often inconclusive. Also, federal support for technology assessment has been cut back in the 1980s. Even if information could be produced, there is likely to be great opposition from the medical community to channeling that information into regulatory action.

On a broader scale, perhaps we could cut out waste by organizing our health care providers into efficient production units. Competitive alternative delivery systems could be the answer. Price competition could send the appropriate signals to squeeze out inefficiency—cut out care that is unnecessary and that provides no net social benefit, perhaps obviating the need for rationing. Henry Aaron estimates that $15 billion to $20 billion a year out of $450 billion spent on national health is wasted on unneeded services. However, Aaron contends that even if we squeeze out all the inefficiency and make the industry operate as efficiently as the best health maintenance organizations (HMOs), the aging of the population and the growth of technology will inevitably lead to additional national expenditures equaling 1 percent of GNP every three or four years. Society may still want to buy the extras and be able to afford them if GNP increases rapidly enough. But more likely not. Discussions of cost containment and rationing, as James Lambrinos pointed out at the conference, must consider the opportunity costs associated with rising health expenditure—the loss of jobs, reduction in standard of living, and price increases.

Determining Probability of Benefit

Although silent on the issue of how societal resources should be allocated generally, William Knaus makes an important statement on how ICU services should be delivered and, by implication, rationed if necessary. Intensive care services should be provided on the basis of medical criteria. Knaus is developing a method of physiologic measurement to estimate the probability of benefiting from intensive care services. To advance the science of prognosis, he recommends a large, nationally based research effort. The probabilities of survival, for example, would be incorporated in the criteria for admission and discharge. Of course, probabilities that are objectively based can be subjectively interpreted. The combination of a low probability of benefit and a poor quality of life, Knaus points out, would for some persons rule out treatment and for others do just the opposite. Furthermore, Knaus acknowledges the possibility of rationing—that demand, for some of the highly complex, expensive care that is available must be modulated by weighing the benefits it would provide to the patient, the resources it would consume, and the unmet demands of other individuals. However, Knaus advises that the professionals keep firm control over the use of probability estimates, to ensure that the rights of the individual are respected and the patient's personal prerogatives and desires are considered.

Although there is a general consensus that it is inappropriate to employ intensive care resources where no purpose is served but the prolongation of the dying process, translating this consensus into practice is very difficult. In the everyday world of the hospital, the crux of the problem is the do-not-resuscitate (DNR) policy. The DNR policy has evolved as part of the consent process that enables clinicians to provide service in accord with the values and desires of their patients. Robert Baker, in tracing the history of DNR policy, notes that the hospital has inverted the standard consent process; instead of seeking consent before treatment, the ICU typically presumes that consent is necessary only when it contemplates ceasing intervention—most notably when it seeks consent not to resuscitate, that is, to issue DNR orders. Conceptually, such activities as cardiopulmonary resuscitation, mechanical ventilation, and nasogastric feeding are interventions equivalent to any other kind of therapy. One does not require consent not to give a therapy.

Because clinicians frequently delay discussing interventions with patients, interventions may continue even though they are not recommended, may not be desired by patients or their families, and may deprive other patients of beneficial resources. The way to correct the defects in DNR policy is to neutralize the built-in procedural bias toward continuing aggressive intervention. To this end Baker recommends the use of advance directives that would allow patients at an early point in their hospitalization to give consent to limit resuscitation interventions in certain circumstances if they should become candidates for the intensive care unit.

Eliminating Marginally Beneficial Services

What is to be done when the number of persons in need of ICU services exceeds the capacity of the unit? Michael Rie explains the formula that he and Tristram Engelhardt developed to deal with such dilemmas. The choice is either to admit more patients and dilute the quality of care or to critically examine the competing claims of early arrivers and newcomers to ICU services. Legal support for the latter position comes from the decision in the *Von Stetina* case, involving an accident victim admitted to an overcrowded ICU who was accidentally disconnected from her ventilator with the result that her brain was deprived of oxygen. During the trial it was pointed out that beds and staff in the ICU could have been freed if two newly arrived patients had been transported to another facility and a near-brain-dead patient transferred to the regular hospital floors.[2]

Engelhardt and Rie use the *Von Stetina* case, successfully argued by the plaintiff, to launch a discussion of an ICU entitlement index. Their index squarely engages the issue of scarce resources by balancing the probability of a successful outcome, the quality of success, and the length of life remaining to a patient against the costs of achieving therapeutic success in the intensive care units. As the costs increase and the quality and likelihood of success decrease, the reasonableness of the investment diminishes. Using the costs of regular care as a gauge, society should judge whether the additional costs of intensive care are justified by the benefits that may be realized (and thus whether to write do-not-resuscitate orders).

Robert M. Veatch, accepting the premise that the marginal benefits of health expenditure may not be worth the marginal costs, has also proposed alternative ways that the marginal medical benefits be cut back—he suggests that we ought to trim the fat and cut into the bone.[3] Veatch explains that the diagnosis-related group (DRG) system is already doing this. He suggests that the DRG system ought to help patients make rational choices. The level of reimbusement should rule out care that is very expensive and only marginally beneficial.

2. *Von Stetina* v. *Florida Medical Center*, 2 Fla. Supp. 2d (Fla. 17 Cir. 1972), 436 Sy. Rptr. 2d 1022 (1983), 10 *Florida Law Weekly*, 286 (Fla., May 24, 1985).

3. Robert M. Veatch, "DRGs and the Ethical Reallocation of Resources," *Hastings Center Report*, June 1986, pp. 32–40.

The rational patient, he argues, would choose a policy of lower reimbursement levels if the money saved were his to spend as he wished.

Clearly Engelhardt and Rie's ICU entitlement index and Veatch's DRG proposal are provocative. Both call on society to explicitly decide, in the form of DRG weights or entitlement index thresholds, on the appropriate levels of investment in resources for intensive care. It is not at all certain that government is ready to face this responsibility.

THE BRITISH EXPERIENCE

With a centralized government and a parliamentary system with strong party discipline, the British control expenditures for health through a system of central and regional budgeting. Aggregate spending in Great Britain is roughly one-half the per capita rate in the United States (with no discernible difference in quality). With 6.5 percent of GNP going to health services, Britain has the lowest rate of medical inflation in the Western democracies. But the British have from one-fifth to one-twentieth as many ICU beds per capita as other Western countries, and some hospitals do not provide intensive care. Dialysis for patients in the final stage of renal disease is generally cut off at the age of fifty-five. As Henry J. Aaron and William B. Schwartz have pointed out in *The Painful Prescription: Rationing Hospital Care* (Brookings, 1984), decisions about the allocation of services on the national and regional level set the premises for the decisions the British physician makes at the bedside. Faced with limited hospital budgets, hospital-based physician-specialists, who are salaried employees of the government and generally have much more clinical autonomy than their American counterparts, ration medical care by dispensing it to those for whom it will do the most good. It is thus the physician, acting as gatekeeper, who makes the trade-offs and makes decisions based on need.

ENTERING THE POLICY ARENA

Many persons in the United States accept the rhetoric of limited resources—the notion that the marginal cost in health care services far outweighs any incremental improvement in health status in terms of what those resources could do if they were used in some other way. But American political institutions generally resist debating the necessity of cutting back beneficial services. Trimming the fat, yes (cutting out nonbeneficial services); but cutting into the bone, never.

There may be good reasons economically for framing the policy debate as a cost-containment issue as opposed to a reduction in beneficial services. There is a lot of fat in the system. But there may be good reasons politically for approaching the assignment of priorities in the use of resources and rationing gingerly and indirectly rather than directly. Controversy is submerged by avoiding the agonizing debates over values and outcomes, which are driven by comprehensive and explicit calculations, and by sticking to changes that are only marginally different from existing policy. Also, small "mistakes" in public policy, brought to the policy arena by ever-attentive interest groups, can easily be repaired. This "muddling through," as Charles E. Lindblom characterizes it, is the sine qua non of incremental policymaking—a decisionmaking style that matches the institutional design of Congress and our national public policymaking apparatus.

Willis Gradison outlines the congressional response to the difficult political and ethical dilemmas arising from the need to meet the three goals of providing access to health care, ensuring the quality of care, and limiting the cost of care. Congress, following the lead of the private sector, intends to use its market power to become a prudent buyer of health services. Relying on competitive systems such as health maintenance organizations (HMOs), Congress can reduce the federal role in defining scope and quality of services. It also has created mechanisms such as peer review organizations and hospital ethics committees to assist physicians in making decisions about life-sustaining therapy.

In the face of a political system that tends to deflect discussion over hard choices, the market may come to play an important role in forcing the difficult value-laden trade-offs that surround rationing decisions. In fact, it is currently fashionable and theoretically appealing to tout the market as the appropriate decisionmaking mechanism for rationing. However, in presenting the third-party perspective, Lindsay Robinson is clearly uncomfortable with what he considers to be the default of policymakers. According to Robinson, in the absence of a well-articulated social policy, a reimbursement policy that is driven by the need to keep costs down can only do a poor job in meeting public expectations.

WHO SHOULD BE THE RATIONER?

Although debate over explicit rationing is still remote from the U.S. political arena, what is not remote is budget cutting and cost containment, which are intended to squeeze inefficiency out of hospitals. But as the impact of budget cutting accumulates over time, hospitals' practices drift in unintended and unpredictable directions. On occasion the financial squeeze results in de facto rationing—which may not be rational and raises questions of who the rationer should be.

The likely candidate is the physician. Robert Veatch, at the conference, warned of the consequences of asking the physician to be society's cost-containment agent, to replace the Hippocratic Oath with a warning, something like this: "I will generally work for your interests, but in the case of marginally beneficial expensive care, I will abandon you in order to serve society as their cost-containment agent." Veatch proposes that only society through its democratic institutions can make such decisions.

But as Aaron points out about the British National Health Service, constrained resources (a relatively small number of ICU beds, for example) force the physician to make the trade-offs. When critical equipment is in limited supply, physicians have to make trade-offs and weigh the benefits for different patients.

American physicians may increasingly find themselves in such a constrained situation. Some intensive care units, especially in large urban areas, are in a state of perpetual triage decisionmaking because they are filled to capacity. Backed-up emergency rooms, beds in the halls, postponed surgery, diluted nurse-patient ratios, and over-stretched facilities are frequently encountered in big city hospitals. Knaus and Baker both suggest that explicit protocols and criteria for admitting and discharging intensive care patients should be adopted by the hospitals to optimize treatment outcomes, contain costs, prevent staff burnout, and reduce liability claims. Daniel Teres, who is on the firing line, presents the perspective of the practicing ICU physician (the "triage officer") who must make the allocational decisions at the bedside.

In the face of pressure to hold costs down there is likely to be increased managerial scrutiny and monitoring of the use of resources, equipment purchases, and staffing levels, and imposition of a formal gate-keeping function with or without explicit admission criteria. Barbara Grumet warns that the legal system will not be of any great assistance in helping physicians make the tough allocational decisions. Constrained ICU resources may very well hasten the emergence of a street-level bureaucracy. Perhaps it is not too far-fetched to predict that the ICU staff of the the future will join the ranks of teachers, social workers, policemen, and lower court judges as what Michael Lipsky calls harassed "street-level bureaucrats." These are the public servants dispensing vital and often life-sustaining services who have great discretion but inadequate resources, involuntary clients, and ambiguous or contradictory performance expectations.

In his summary commentary, Michael Rie recognizes the plight of the physician decisionmaker—"squeezed" by the patient's rights to consumption on one side and cost containment and decreased resources on the other side—whom society has failed to provide with any policy to guide him in his allocation of services. Rie's answer is to call for a wide-ranging societal discussion (conceptualized as the public creation of an ICU entitlement index) of the issue of critical care—of what should be expected from expenditures and the choice and priorities that should govern the allocation of ICU resources. The proposals for reform by four of the participants drawn up after the conference on rationing of medical care for the critically ill should help to advance this discussion.

Ethics and Scarcity

Scarcity in health delivery services in the United States comes out of abundance. It is because we as a nation have had the means by which we can push against the limits of disease that we have now reached an impasse. Where there are no artificial hearts, or no means by which implantation is possible, one is not able to talk about who has the claim on the procedures and techniques that might extend the life of a heart-diseased patient.

Technical and scientific skills and the ability to pay for research into medical areas that could hardly have been dreamed of before have brought us to this curious impasse. We have the increasing ability to push back against those limits we had thought to be absolute. But the cost of our applied science in its technology and the cost of delivering the benefits of technology are becoming more and more clear. The cost of delivery of renal dialysis, for example, gives one pause when one considers any technological advances as an entitlement and a right.

Scarcity in critical care and in the delivery services for the critically ill is a scarcity that arises from the social question of affordability when the claims for medical advances are set alongside the many other needs that lead to social well-being. The amount of money and resources that can be allocated to critical care is at this level a national economic question which also becomes a political question. The citizen might have a right to the best care available, under an abstract principle of justice. But the issue of availability is not simply an abstract question. Rights are determined by availability, and availability is determined by cultural and social claims which are themselves in competition with one another. Abstract moral judgments in the area of allocation of resources are easy to come by but add more heat than light to the solution of the dilemmas present. Allocation of resources across the whole field of social concerns and demands is a question that must be raised before any question of distribution of what is to be allocated to any particular area of concern can be answered.

The question of affordability in health care has been brought to our attention by the federal government's institution of a system for controlling payments under medicare. The DRG, or diagnosis-related group, system represents a national political decision on how funds are to be allocated for health care. This judgment about the limits of what can be allocated can press on us the need to look at how the funds that have been allocated can be distributed equitably—that is, at rationing.

Rationing presupposes scarcity along with a principle of distribution that emphasizes both need and equitability. Any rationing system must recognize the differences in need that set up priorities for distribution. Only after the priority needs are fulfilled does equitability take over. A part of the ethical question that arises from rationing, therefore, comes from the examination of the way in which one determines the priority of needs.

But before considering any question of allocation or rationing, one has to ask whether there are ethical issues that arise in the use of resources for critical care apart from the question of scarcity. If we could have as many intensive care units (ICUs) as were needed to meet demand, would there still be a series of ethical questions that could be raised over the use of ICUs?

One has, of course, to examine the use of ICUs under practical circumstances before one can make a general rule. However, a case can be made that, faced with the presence of a unit that can deal with failure of critical organs, there is an impulse to do everything and anything to stave off death. There are ethical issues that have to be dealt with when one is faced with "pulling the plug" and in using ICUs in very advanced cases where there is little prospect of a patient's survival.

The shortage of machines is not at issue in dealing with the problems posed by cases like that of Karen Quinlan. The nature of the machines themselves seems sometimes to insulate us from the normal progress of our dying. Here ethical issues center around the way we recognize the nature of our personhood, our being as persons. In our secular, pluralistic society the tragedy is that we do not have a clearly held view about the nature of self-hood. Indeed the recognition of "death always as a disaster," to use Paul Ramsey's phrase, arises from our cultural failure to have a clear picture of the self within the world. Ours is an age when we are forever looking at the social origins of our institutions but rarely asking the important reflective Socratic question, "How should one live?"

Because we look at death as a disaster, with little in our secularized world to give us a way of responding to the fact of death with integrity, we tend to use machines to provide us with some last hope. The machines, in a curious way, can become the ethical problem.

The development of a technology of rescue in critical cases has brought a new dimension of care as well as a new level of care. Because of the nature of the elements of the technology used, the nature of treatment has significantly changed; what had seemed fundamental as the basic tenets of doctor-patient relationships are no longer sufficient. To promote health is a positive claim on a physician. In intensive care units, the question often is not the promotion of health but the maintenance of life, with health a secondary issue. The nature of the technology can change both the way in which the doctor perceives the patient and the context within which treatment is offered. The former change is brought about by the interjection of a highly sophisticated technological system which involves significant teamwork by professionals along with the physician. The patient tends to become no more than a player in a very complicated game—often a game played for its own sake. Whatever else occurs, the sense of the patient as a person whose health is at issue tends to be lost, or at least significantly minimized.

The change in the context of the treatment occurs because the technology places cost at the center of the picture, whether one likes it or not. In a unit offering critical care, the doctor with his patient-centered view is but one player who works alongside other players who might have cost management and priority management at the center of their concerns.

The understanding of the use of ICUs that arises from the many points of view involved, the fear of death that drives us to create more and more defenses against our own death, combined with the tendency of the technology to make the care impersonal and to focus on the use of technology for its own sake, encourages abuse. It creates an artificial demand and thus a scarcity which demands some form of rationing.

What scarcity does is to make the ethical issue that arises with the use of the intensive care unit more acute. It forces us to ask the ethical and moral questions. But even here the issue is not as direct as it would seem. We are left wondering whether we could have avoided the choices which arise out of scarcity by exercising better management and control. Is it the physician who should bear the burden of decision in this kind of conflict? Should the physician be involved in the management decision that leads to the conflict?

It is important to note that the nature of the question has been changed. I have argued that there is a question about the use of the intensive care units or life-prolonging machines (which prolong death rather than life) that has precedence over the problems raised by scarcity. That question centers on the integrity of the person. Is something of humanness lost under some uses of the ICUs—for example, when they are used simply to prolong death? The physician in a situation of scarcity who faces the question of prolonging death is filled with his sense of duty to do all that can be done for the patient and, one fears, for concern about what will happen if he is sued for not placing the patient under intensive care.

The latter concern is one that pushes itself more and more into the equation, as physicians face the possibility of the "second guess" from an inconsistent source and thus are tempted to do all that is mechanically necessary to show that all steps were taken for survival. Yet another extraneous element has intruded itself between doctor and patient, making the patient less a person to be treated than a problem to be dealt with, given certain objective circumstances.

The legal threat poses an interesting question. Any legal argument against a physician must rest on the notion that everything reasonable that needs to be done for survival must be done. But the more complicated the procedures used in intensive care, the more difficult it is to decide what is reasonable care. In fact, with the confusion of roles between physician and hospital administrator, one is left with both the confusion of who is to determine what is reasonable and the haunting specter of the inconsistent "second guess." This added factor can only increase the cost of an already costly system. The use of the system is forced beyond what is reasonable and often beyond the best interests of the patient. One has only to look at the use of tests, ad nauseam, without regard to patients' interest or to reason but asked for in order to defend against malpractice claims, to see the probable abuse of the more expensive systems of care.

In a country where there has been very little experience of conscious rationing of health care, we are being pushed by cultural forces to acknowledge its necessity. The allocation of resources by the federal government, our fear of death, the unwillingness of physicians to acknowledge the fact of mortality when it seems like defeat, the legal pressure to do the utmost, even when the utmost is not best for the patient, all push toward the recognition of a scarcity of resources for technological rescue apparatus. Apart from any moral question that arises over treating the patient as a person, one is forced into questions about the distribution of a scarce resource.

I have noted the place that the threat of malpractice can play in the doctor-patient relationship. But it also plays a part in increasing costs. Anyone with the remotest contact with a hospital is aware of the cost implication of malpractice suits. Curiously enough, if one were to look at the legal issues involved, apart from the use of the law in its punitive aspects, one might find a clue to the moral issues that must be faced in the issue of rationing.

Because lawyers make their fees in negligence cases contingent on the damages awarded, they are able to press suit for damages in cases where the patients have no means to do so on their own. One thing made possible by the contingency fee system is the opening of the legal game to rich and poor alike. The possibility thus exists that legal questions will be raised on the outcome of any procedural use of intensive care treatment. Those who have the responsibility to make decisions about intensive care have the obligation to base them either on equitability or on a carefully agreed upon prospectus of needs.

I am not arguing that we should turn to the law for an answer to our moral problems in dealing with rationing. Rather, we should recognize that this process of law does clarify the issues. The questions that have to be addressed are: (1) Have we done all that is reasonably expected for the patient? (2) Have we treated this particular patient equitably? (3) Have we an established protocol for dealing with a group of patients competing for scarce resources? (4) Does that protocol recognize diversity of needs, apart from the principle of equitability? This framework raises fundamental questions, but it is here that the moral issues peep through. What is the relationship between equitability and a set of acceptable standards of social needs? What is equitability in health care? Where there is a shortage of sugar, you can give less sugar to everyone, but you do not just give everyone less health care. Some get intensive care, but others do not.

The last of the four questions makes it clear that a protocol used to decide between cases is essential. The moral issue is not equitability alone, but who can best be treated. Equitability itself would seem to demand that we look beyond it to an understanding of the relationship between patient and treatment results, taking away the impulse to think of this kind of treatment as a "last chance effort."

In all of these questions two principles emerge as of fundamental importance. National allocations force questions of rationing on us, yet the ethical questions must be faced with the quality of care of the patient and the patient's quality of life in mind.

MAX HARRY WEIL

Alternatives to Rationing

This conference is considering the rationing of medical care for the critically ill. I prefer to consider the alternatives to rationing. In terms of my assessment of the risks and rewards in the delivery of intensive care services, the pertinent question is, are we dealing with a scarcity of resources? My answer is an unequivocal no. But are we dealing with an inappropriateness in the use of our resources? My answer to that question is an unequivocal yes. In order to insert some concept of how to right the system, I am going to discuss how the physician, who is at the front end of this system, can decide whether his care of the critically ill is governed by the three Rs—is his care rational, redeeming, and respectful?

Before I discuss alternatives, I must point out how intensive care technology is being used and what the benefits and the risks of that technology are, and the implications that stem therefrom with regard to the appropriateness of use. Then I come right back to my three Rs as a tool with which I can approach appropriate use of that technology by health professionals at the bedside.

In the twenty-five years since this area of medicine has developed, the use of elaborately instrumented, sophisticated life support technology has become routine. Technology has made it possible to do remarkable things—to stop and start the heart; to let an individual who has lost his kidney functions survive; to allow one who would otherwise die because he cannot breathe to breathe; and even to transplant hearts and implant hearts.

In some ways technology has far outdistanced the compassionate, admittedly limited, armamentarium of the family physician. The transition from the compassionate care of yesteryear has not been easy, either for society or for the health professional. The ethical, legal, and economic pressures that stem from the change are largely unresolved. When we are in trouble, we tend to turn to ethics and

17

to religion. The Judeo-Christian ethic holds that life is to be preserved at all costs. For example, Deuteronomy 30:19 counsels: "I have set before you life, that both thou and thy seed may live." The young physician at the bedside quite predictably responds: "We must do something or the patient will die." The assumption is that the act itself will turn the tide and maintain life. Questions about the duration or the quality of life are ignored.

It is the very existence of the technology that motivates its use. Do something. "Have hammer; will pound." "Have scissors; will cut."

We monitor the critically ill very carefully. It is informative. It helps in making decisions. But it is also invasive of the patient's body, demanding sophisticated equipment, high skill, and expensive hospitalization. Yet it also fails, as technology may, and it is not without risk. For instance, one of the widely used tools for monitoring in an intensive care unit is the so-called Swan-Ganz catheter which is inserted into a vein, usually in the neck, and allowed to float, balloon-like, into the pulmonary artery. It provides us with some very helpful information not otherwise available. But in 2–3 percent of all cases, when that catheter floats into the pulmonary artery, it obstructs the flow of blood to the lungs and produces a pulmonary infarct—death of lung tissue which, under conditions of other critical illness, may of itself curtail the patient's chance of survival.

Such catheters, if kept in place for six days, not only begin to lose their utility but to cause a variety of complications, such as infections and blood clots. And the cost of keeping the catheters in place for six days is estimated to be 2 percent of the patient's life—a 2 percent chance of death due to infection from the catheter alone, after six days.

Clearly technology can be costly in human as well as financial terms, a problem that has come under close scrutiny in recent years. This has been especially true in the newer, more technologically oriented specialties, such as intensive care medicine. So it was that in 1983 the National Institutes of Health called a consensus development conference to find out what is real about the practice of intensive care medicine. One of the conclusions was: "Monitoring of critically ill patients is a highly expensive component of intensive care. It is easy to assume a proportional relationship between the quantity of information and the quality of care, but this is not necessarily true."[1] I think that many physicians subscribe to that statement.

The net effect of monitoring a variable that is not important in decisionmaking would be the sum total of the complications of the resulting therapy, plus any direct complications from the mode of monitoring itself. Therefore, the existence of the technology—"Have scissors; will cut"—is not synonymous with benefit to the individual patient.

A tracheostomy—cutting a hole into the trachea to place a breathing tube in it—is a procedure that is not new, but it involves some hazards. When it results in prolonged artificial ventilation of patients, complications can be very serious. It is true that the underlying diseases of such patients have a high mortality, but it is estimated that as much as 10 percent of the risk of death is encountered from the tracheostomy alone over a period of three months.

Some even more major technological interventions that are sometimes redeeming often are not. For example, in the placement of a balloon into the aorta, the major blood vessel of the body, to take the workload off the heart, complications occur in 16 percent of all cases. That would be acceptable if the balloon pumping of itself was expected to save lives; but it is combined with a surgical procedure, and usually after the patient has suffered a heart attack.

What does the NIH consensus development conference say about survival, then? Evidence is equivocal, but the weight of clinical opinion is that intensive care improves the chances of survival. It is recognized, however, that for some patients the risks of iatrogenic illnesses associated with that care may outweigh any potential benefit. That is the concept to which I am exposing you.

In 1970 in a very large intensive care service in Los Angeles— perhaps the first intensive care service in the country—we began to track mortality of patients admitted into our units. Between 1970 and 1980 we could show no improvement in overall survival. That was astounding, for that was the era of the Swan-Ganz catheter, of remarkably new capabilities for artificial breathing, and of major improvements in antibiotics for the control of infection.

By measuring the lactic acid content of blood, we could estimate

---

1. Jospeh E. Parrillo and Steven M. Ayres, eds., *Major Issues in Critical Care Medicine* (Baltimore: Williams and Wilkins, 1984), pp. 277–89.

whether the severities of illness at the time of patient admission in 1980 in terms of circulatory defect were comparable to those in 1970. We found no difference in severity between the two years.

I do not believe there is any likelihood that we have not improved our life-saving techniques. I have no doubt that in certain conditions the Swan-Ganz catheter, the balloon pump, and tracheostomy are life saving. But iatrogenic complications—those introduced by the physician—have robbed us of our profit, and overall performance has not necessarily improved.

This is the context in which we should discuss the rationing of medical care for the critically ill. The intensive care unit, I believe, combines the capacity to provide needed care and technology with the potential to do great harm.

Some of what I am discussing is not new. A prestigious American medical scientist, Robert Austrian, in a classical paper in 1964 stated that antimicrobial therapy—that is, antibiotic therapy—has little or no effect on the outcome of infection among those destined at the onset of illness to die within five days.[2] Pneumonia is the old man's blessing, and we do not change it even with our potent drugs. The same applies under some circumstances to patients with advanced malignant diseases.

If we are going to be both ethically and religiously inclined, in discussing these issues, we can find help in Ecclesiastes 3:1–2: "To everything there is a season, and a time to every purpose under the heaven; a time to be born, and a time to die; a time to plant, and a time to pluck up that which is planted." We are not very successful, even with our very impressive high technology, in resurrecting that for which we have no option.

The depersonalization that high technology promotes—the heroics of "Have hammer; will pound" and "Have scissors; will cut"—is not in concert with the wishes of the society we serve. My daughter, a nurse in an intensive care unit at a university hospital, told a hopeless, nightmare story in which the hardest part was getting the patient's family to let go, accept death, and turn off the machinery. Just as the family decided to do so a resident physician offered them just one more thing to do.

2. Robert Austrian and Jerome Gold, "Pneumococcal Bacteremia with Especial Reference to Bacteremic Pneumococcal Pneumonia," *Annals of Internal Medicine*, vol. 60, no. 2 (1964), pp. 759–76.

There are profound legal issues involved in such decisions. But the law has always followed, not preceded, the identification of the problem, as these headlines make clear: "Brain Dead Youth Dies as Parents Plead with Docs to Pull the Plug"; "Child Taken off Respirator Despite Family Plea, the Doctor Testifies"; "Respirator Unplugged; Two Doctors Held for Murder by the District Attorney of Los Angeles County."

This story tugs at my heartstrings. Ten years ago, I was taking care of a thirty-five-year-old man who was dying of lung cancer. He was bleeding to the point that he could not breathe. His airway was filling with blood, and I was manipulating a bronchoscope. I was part of that group that said, "We must act." When I cleared his airway, he asked for a pad of paper and wrote, "Everything is over; leave me alone." Technology and patient advocacy. Where does the scale tip?

In this light, I ask what it is that you want to limit. The types of diseases that are eligible for treatment? The age beyond which a patient is not eligible? The liability issues so that doctors can practice more cost-effective medicine? What is it that we are to ration?

Is the question whether we should ration so that we must determine who shall live and who shall die? Is that really the problem that is before us? I submit that it is not.

Some time ago my daughter, who is an attorney, and I developed what we called a checklist of the three Rs—rational, redeeming, and respectful—that, if appropriately utilized, would do away with the need of rationing as we have defined it.

Is there a biological rationale for the intervention either diagnostic or therapeutic? And, if there is a rationale, is it redeeming? Is it effective to get to an appropriate endpoint? And that endpoint may not only be immediate survival; it may be intermediate survival and quality of life. Is it respectful of the individual? Does it respect the rights of the patient?

There is no rationale in treating a 95 percent body burn in a sixty-five-year-old man because there has never been a sixty-five-year-old man with a 95 percent body burn who has survived. Neither is it unethical, even though it is not rational, to attempt to sustain such an individual. No 250-gram infant fetus—half a pound or less—has survived after birth. Do we expend what have been referred to as scarce resources to try to do once what has never been done, and particularly under conditions that are uncontrolled? If you have a carcinoma of the pancreas with metastases to the brain, do you operate on the abdomen or the brain?

There is no survival. It is not rational; therefore, you need go no further.

The next question is, is it redeeming? It may be rational. You clutch your chest with a pain due to coronary artery disease—angina pectoris—and that pain is due to a single-vessel obstruction of one of the three coronary arteries. There is no proof that coronary artery surgery, or even percutaneous transluminal coronary angioplasty, done through a catheter, is redeeming in terms of prolongation of life. It may bring comfort, but the vast majority of coronaries can be controlled by medication without the risk, pain, and cost of surgery. The weight of evidence is that we do a horrendous number of coronary bypass operations in this country every year that do not meet the test of rational or redeeming.

The same thing applies to the insertion of a catheter, like the Swan-Ganz catheter, for six days, with a 2 percent mortality from the catheter alone. Is it redeeming? In some instances, it may be. In the vast majority of instances, it is not.

And, is it respectful? Does it respect the patient's desires and his decisions? That enters into living will and durable powers. Do we respect the patient's wish to discontinue therapy?

If it does not make sense, it is not rational. If it does not have reasonable likelihood of benefit in relation to the risks, then it is not effective or redeeming. And, if it is not respectful, it is improper; it violates the moral and the legal rights of the patient. My daughter and I have put together an addendum to the three Rs that we call QC. The three Rs require no ethics committee, no judge at the bedside; those decisions can be made on site. A small minority of issues that are more complex and that involve the quality of life or the policy and legal decisions that have to do with cost are beyond the reach of the individual physician. We recognize those. We call them the QCs. They are the issues for which we need the Queen's Counsel, the additional help of ethics committees or alternate means of support representing the larger capabilities and interests of society.

The questions that we ask of the counsel are: Is it right for the patient in human terms? For an individual who cannot speak for himself, is it compatible with the priorities of the patient if he could speak for himself and the family and the society in which he lives?

Is the monetary value of risk and reward rational for the patient, for the family, for the society?

Those are questions that cannot be answered by the physician alone, by the health provider alone. They are answered by a larger representation of society.

If we apply the concept inherent in the three Rs—rational, redeeming, and respectful—the limited resources (or the scarce resources, as they have been referred to) would be unlikely to be scarce. Therefore, what would be the rationale of conventional rationing concepts, with the implication that we will decide who will live and who will die? What we need to do is to make sure that the resources are appropriately allocated.

For that, I suggest that if it is rational, redeeming, and respectful, the resources that we presently have will be a plenty.

Lessons from the United Kingdom

Rationing is an issue that we are going to have to face, but not necessarily a course we are going to decide to follow.

Although the arithmetic and the logic of rationing are straightforward, I do not think the issue is well understood by the general public. We face an extremely difficult economic, social trade-off. For about three decades now per capita and real—that is, inflation-adjusted—expenditures for medical care have been going up 5–6 percent a year. There is no indication that the technological creativity that has been largely responsible for the very rapid growth in medical outlays is abating. Scientific imagination, which has given us various kinds of transplants and the new methods of treatment and diagnosis that have been driving up expenditures, is likely to push even harder in the future. Nor is the population getting younger. While the proportion of the population over sixty-five years old is growing slowly, those over seventy-five and especially over eighty-five are increasing very rapidly as a proportion of the population and will continue to do so for the next forty to fifty years.

The implication of these two factors—the continuing fecundity of scientific imagination, the continuing aging of the population—is that the forces underlying the growth in medical expenditures in the past two to three decades will remain strong. I am not dismissing the point that some medical care is unnecessary and may provide no net social benefit. Nor am I ignoring the proposition that hospitals, in many cases, could be more efficiently run than they are now, although the statement would have carried more weight five years ago than it does today. I am suggesting, however, that unnecessary care does not, in any significant measure, account for the growth in total spending on medical care.

With health accounting for something over 10 percent of gross national product, do we wish to continue paying the bill? Do we wish to continue facing annual increases in expenditure on the order of 6 percent a year after adjustment for inflation? Anything that grows 6 percent a year doubles in real terms about every twelve years. Our GNP has not been doing that, but spending on health care has. If we continue on that trend we would be spending about another 1 percent of gross national product every three to four years.

The debate over rising medical costs, and whether we wish to pay for them, can only intensify. The question now is whether it is possible to slow the rate of growth of medical spending purely by eliminating wasteful outlays—by squeezing out defensive medicine through reform of malpractice insurance, for example—by more efficient operation of hospitals, perhaps by running the entire medical sector with the efficiency now attained by the best-run health maintenance organizations in the United States.

Such an effort to squeeze out waste can, at best, only temporarily slow the rate of growth of spending for medical care. The effort to squeeze out that waste is immensely important, however. Because of the importance and size of medical care, the social loss from wasting medical resources is huge—on the order of $15 billion to $20 billion, perhaps even $25 billion, a year in resources that could be saved with little, if any, loss in overall medical efficiency and medical care.

But that number is small by comparison with the annual increases in medical outlays. Even if we were able to squeeze out all inefficiency, all waste, and make the entire fee-for-service medical care sector run as cheaply as the best-run health maintenance organizations, the best we could hope is that the proportion of gross national product devoted to medical care would level off for three to four years. Given the imperfect world in which we live, the likelihood of eliminating the cost differential between the fee-for-services sector and health maintenance organizations with no loss of medical benefits is rather small.

More likely there will be a brief period, like the one in 1985, during which medical expenditures—hospital outlays in particular—rise relatively slowly. Then, once again, the very pressures that have been driving outlays up for two to three decades will reassert themselves and we will face the question anew—how much of this additional outlay is purchasing medical care that is worth the cost?

It is quite possible that we will conclude that all of it is worth the cost. And if we want to pursue that course, we have the economic resources to do so. With modest growth in gross national product—3 percent a year, say, in real terms—we can buy everything that medical technology can offer us, even if spending on health care grows as fast as it has for the last two to three decades. And we can continue to have at least as much left over for other outlays of personal consumption as we have had in the past. We will not have to cut consumption to pay for medical expenditures. Conceivably our political, social, and ethical judgments will lead us to buy all beneficial medical care. However, as outlays rise, the issue of whether to ration will be presented to the nation ever more vigorously, and we may well decide that we do not want to buy everything for everybody that the medical care sector is capable of producing.

Rationing would raise very difficult problems. The nature of the choices that would have to be faced, should we decide to pursue that course, can be gathered from the model that William Schwartz[1] and I have explored, namely, Great Britain's medical care system.[1] To be sure, rationing goes on rather fiercely in the United Kingdom because per capita expenditures on hospital care are on the order of half of what they are in the United States.

The differences between Britain and the United States are large. What sorts of results will ensue if the medical care profession is forced by a lack of resources to curtail drastically the quantity of services it is able to provide? In many respects we were surprised by what we found. Some things are not rationed at all in Britain. Such procedures as the treatment for hemophilia seemed to be provided just as frequently in Britain and at as high a level as in the United States. Radiation therapy for cancer is provided at a level similar to that in the United States. Chemotherapy for cancers where responsiveness to such treatment has been demonstrated seems to be provided about as often as in the United States.

Hip replacement, much written about because of the very lengthy queues for surgery, is provided almost as often in Britain as in the United States. But because those suffering from chronic hip disease survive, even a small shortfall will, after a time, generate a large queue. As a result, people in Great Britain sometimes wait for lengths of time that I think would be regarded as intolerable in the United States.

More striking, however, are the therapies that are drastically rationed in Great Britain. Coronary artery surgery is done about a

1. Henry J. Aaron and William B. Schwartz, *The Painful Prescription: Rationing Hospital Care* (Brookings, 1984).

tenth as often as in the United States. The National Institutes of Health have suggested that we probably do too much, that perhaps 30 percent of coronary artery surgery could be replaced with medical therapy. If we reduced our surgery accordingly, that would leave the United States doing five to six times more coronary surgery than Britain.

About a third as many people with chronic renal failure will receive dialysis in the United Kingdom as in the United States. The CAT scanner is used in about a fifth as many diagnoses, on a per capita basis, as in the United States. And for cancers where the effectiveness of chemotherapy has not been thoroughly documented, a great deal less chemotherapy is administered in Great Britain than in the United States. Many physicians would argue that withholding such therapy is not a case of rationing but a humane and sensible medical care that recognizes the unpleasant side effects of chemotherapy.

The pattern of rationing that we observed in Britain, and the explanations that we encountered scores of times in interviews with physicians, medical care planners, and people from the private sector, suggest that in the face of externally imposed limits on resources, the providers of health care change their values. They adopt different standards for what is medically appropriate, much as physicians during wartime make medical judgments—triage decisions—that they would not make if resources and time were freely available. This point was made in a variety of ways by physicians. One, for example, indicated that in order to sleep well at night, in order to be at peace with their professional lives, physicians have to recognize that they are acting in their capacity as social agents administering the resources that politically have been determined to be available for health care. They have to find explanations for themselves as to why, in certain cases, medical therapy is not indicated.

The most striking example of this incorporation of value judgments came in a discussion with a nephrologist. In Britain, at the time of our interviews, it was standard procedure not to provide dialysis for people with renal failure who were over fifty-five years old, and in regions with poor resources the age limit tended to be lower. Why, we asked, would a patient with chronic renal failure but no other major problems be turned away? The physician's reply: "Oh, but you have to understand—everybody over the age of fifty-five is a bit crumbly."

This was a terse and somewhat ironic—though not intended to be ironic—description of the attitudes and points of view that emerged. Another nephrologist referred, much more seriously and persuasively, to the physicians' need, in order to function psychologically in the face of limited resources, to look for indications not to give treatment in cases where resources are not available. In plainer language, they need criteria on which to base what are essentially triage decisions.

From our American as well as our British experience, we concluded that it is simply impossible for physicians and patients, both with adequate resources at their disposal, to exercise economy. If any significant savings are to be achieved, they must occur because of externally imposed constraints that force decisions on patients and physicians. The most dramatic instances are apparent in difficulties that the British have with any procedure that can be provided out of generally available hospital resources. If all it takes are regular supplies from the pharmacy, operating room time, standard nursing care, normal equipment, and a physician's observation and participation in planning care, it is very hard to curtail the amount of care.

British physicians all responded in the same way to the case that we described to them of a young man about twenty-five years old who was very seriously injured in an automobile accident and sent to a small community hospital where resources and perhaps expertise were lacking. His condition worsened drastically, and he was transferred to a major teaching hospital. His chance of survival was judged to be very, very small. But the nature of his injuries and problems was such that if he did survive, his recovery would be complete, so that he could resume normal life without significant impairment.

The hospital spent $100,000 in the unsuccessful attempt to save this young man's life. Simple arithmetic says that if you have one hundred such patients, each with a 1 percent chance of surviving, and you spend $100,000 on each, it will cost $10 million on the average to save one life. Surely, confronted with this kind of situation, in a resource-limited system, they would try to save money. Not so. Every physician responded, without exception, that at a British teaching hospital everything would be done to try and save the patient's life. In that situation, the resources are available. They are made available in emergencies, and no rationing will be done with respect to available resources.

What does it take to induce rationing? It takes an externally imposed constraint within which physicians have to adjust. It takes the failure to build additional hospitals, the failure to maintain additional beds, the failure to purchase the equipment necessary to do certain specialized kinds of surgical procedures. It takes a vacancy in the staff for a cardiologist to hold down the number of coronary artery bypass grafts that will be performed. In short, somebody has to make a decision that either the equipment or the personnel will not be available to do something, thereby forcing the remaining staff to exercise the kinds of choices that I described.

While I think the British experience is instructive for the United States, Britain is not a template for what the United States will face, if we should decide to slow the growth of medical spending and thus significantly force some kinds of rationing decisions. For a variety of reasons, Britain is different from the United States, and our experience would not mirror theirs.

One of the most important differences is the political system. The British budgetary limits for medical care are determined within a parliamentary system marked by party discipline. When the government decides what the budget will be, it is adopted. The government may be thrown out, but thus far limits on the National Health Service have not proven salient political issues in any campaign.

The political process in the United States in recent years has not been marked by party discipline, or discipline of almost any kind. Consequently, the chances that we would successfully enforce limits as stringent as those in Britain seem vanishingly small. Recall the experience when insurance companies and state regulatory agencies tried to slow the process of automatically paying for liver transplants. It was not long before members of Congress called hearings. The evening news contained photographs of infants who were suffering from congenital liver disease. And, to cap matters, the White House appointed a special assistant to help coordinate the efforts of various families to obtain liver transplants. The financial walls came tumbling down.

We are not going to face limits as stringent as those in Britain, at least for the foreseeable future, because we do not have the political stomach for it.

Other differences mean that the road would be a great deal rockier and that we would proceed less far down it. The aggressiveness of U.S. patients is well remarked, and it is reinforced by their tendency to go to the courts. Physicians in the United States still do the majority of operations on a fee-for-service basis, whereas in Britain specialists are largely salaried and hospital-based.

Each of those factors means that the United States is likely to be more careful—or perhaps less bold, to phrase it differently—in marching down the cost-containment road. But if we do decide to save money on a sustained basis, the past year's experience suggests that we shall begin to impose restrictions of various kinds. The first step is to try to scale back on procedures, on care, on outlays that we regard as really of negligible benefit. We try to let patients out early, to save costs on those later and less beneficial days. Hospitals are somewhat more careful in deciding what equipment they are going to purchase. Physicians are subject to peer pressures that they have not known in previous years. The standards of care in the United States, the medical judgments about what to do and when, have begun in an embryonic form to change.

But, so far, the limits that we have faced in the United States have been sufficiently mild that we have not had to make significant decisions about rationing. Only in cases where people have made bad mistakes, either medically or in public relations, have things happened that do not look good at all. By and large, the limits imposed have been relatively mild, and in some areas, for some hospitals, the limits that the DRG (diagnosis-related group) system has imposed are the best financial news they have had in years. Hospitals' experience varies with the part of the country they are in, the type of hospital, the patient mix, and so on.

As the technological imperative and the aging of the population begin to reassert themselves, and after we have eliminated all the waste we can, we once again will face the trend growth in medical outlays of 5–6 percent a year that has persisted for about four decades. The only way that we can slow that trend rate of growth will be to confront the kinds of decisions that the British have been encountering for quite a while. When we reach that point I think it is very likely that we will look at the cost and say, "A lot of what we are spending brings benefits—positive, to be sure—but not as great as the costs of the services provided." And we will continue to explore methods of screening out those activities whose costs we judge, as a nation, to be in excess of the benefits they provide.

If that happens, the process is going to have to be one in which budgets and resources for medical care are limited externally so that the providers, within the bounds of medical judgment, can determine which uses have the highest priorities. In the end, the imposition of budget limits should, if anything, heighten the importance and the centrality of the decisions of physicians about what care is to be provided, to whom, and in what types of settings.

Discussion

MICHAEL A. RIE: I have a question that concerns esophageal cancer in the United States and Great Britain and the issue of macroallocation. Dr. Augenstein has referred to the very high mortality in that disease and in considering major cost or financial constraints imposed on the intensive care system, he raised the provocative question, Do I operate?

I have had a lot of experience comparing esophageal surgery in the United States and Great Britain, and I would submit that, for the surgeon, the issue of whether to operate is the same in both countries. But for the American intensive care system the issue is very different from the British. Thoracic surgical residents in England tell me they take the tracheal tube out after twenty-four hours. In American surgical ICUs, that would not be the standard. Some people will go on with airway management for weeks and months. Dr. Augenstein tells us about people lying around the ICU forty-five days after an esophagectomy without any decision being made on where to put them. I would like a little policy-oriented debate on this point between Dr. Augenstein and Dr. Aaron.

JEFFREY S. AUGENSTEIN: I think we are reasonably aggressive about discontinuing therapy, but nowhere near what Britain or other places that have many fewer resources do. There are agonizing decisions. Each one is taken as an individual decision. I think we probably are as aggressive in considering surgery, as aggressive in discontinuing therapy, as we can be. If you look at the ICU at any given point, you will see a number of people who have been there for a number of days with complications of esophageal carcinoma. I don't know how to tell a patient before surgery that he can't have surgery, and I don't know how to stop on day one.

HENRY J. AARON: I think this is one area where the differences in resource availability do have some implications for intensive care and for critical care medicine. American hospitals have about 5 percent of their beds devoted to intensive care. Advanced teaching hospitals may have 10 percent or more. The average in Britain is about 1 percent. At one of the world-famous London teaching hospitals, out of eight hundred beds there are ten ICU beds. As Dr. Schwartz and I reported, the head of that ICU facility—a man of extraordinary devotion and intense care about his activities; a man who lives at the hospital and who has built his own equipment—we thought was a sitting duck. If we asked him whether he shouldn't have more resources, he would say, "Yes, by all means." "No," he said, "it would be out of place in Britain. I have about the right amount of resources for this setting."

ROBERT M. VEATCH: I find it puzzling that clinicians are agonizing over these kinds of choices, particularly about making this choice before you know what the patient's outcome is going to be.

But clinicians, it seems to me, are inevitably in a moral bind. They are either imposing their own value framework on patients, which they ought not to be doing in the 1980s, or, even worse, they are functioning as society's agents to limit the welfare of their patients. It seems to me that is the wrong way of going about it, whether it is before we transfer a patient into a critical situation or not. For the patient with the esophageal cancer or any of the other critically ill patients that we have been talking about, the obvious and straight-forward and first step is to ask the patient or the agent for the patient whether the patient wants the care. If the patient says no, the question is settled, as far as I can see, ethically, legally, financially, in almost all cases, in every other way.

If the patient does want the care, then it surely can't be the clinician's job to be the gatekeeper and keep him from getting the care that he wants. There is nothing in the history of Western medical ethics that would justify a clinician cutting off a patient who wants the care.

If you have to cut off care that the patient wants, it has got to be a societal judgment made by the moral community. For example, I don't know why we don't have a DRG reimbursement of zero for patients who have been in a persistent vegetative state for more than three months, just the way we have a reimbursement of zero for transplant patients under medicare. It ought not to be up to the clinician to try to figure out whether eliminating care on a patient in a persistent vegetative state is doing any good or saving society money. Some physicians who really believe it does good will order the care to continue, and others who believe it doesn't do any good will say it should stop. As far as I can see, that is the physician abandoning the patient's perspective and not doing what ought to be done with regard to the patient.

I don't see how if you formulate the problem in this fashion, you are ever going to get a morally satisfactory answer. It is not the way the question ought to be put.

AARON: I want to suggest that Professor Veatch starts from a very correct position but reaches perhaps an incorrect perspective on what the role of a physician is and should be and certainly will be. The correct observation is that the physician is acting as the agent for the patients that the physician serves. That is where the physician's loyalty belongs.

The problem, however, is that the physician and the patient operate within an overall system and subject to certain constraints. I am not sure that Professor Veatch would disagree with where I am going to be heading. Given the nature of those restrictions and constraints, if resources are limited, the physician must look at trade-offs and benefits of using resources for different patients in his or her care. There is no way, then, to avoid those kinds of weightings and value judgments as among different patients, as among the relative benefits of doing this test for this patient or doing this test for some other patient.

If critical equipment is in limited supply so that there are queues, so that not all physicians can get on this machine as much or as often as they would like, then trade-offs have to be made and benefits for different patients have to be weighed.

So, I think the moral imperative is there, and it should be there and it always will be there, as long as physicians are devoted to their service as they are. But that is going to force them precisely in the direction of weighing benefits and costs of doing things for different people.

VEATCH: Dr. Aaron and I, I think, are quite close. We certainly agree that the clinician ought to remain as the patient advocate, but I don't see how he can then go on to say that this requires that the physician look at trade-offs. Insofar as the physician is reducing or eliminating care in order to benefit his patient, that fits with the advocacy role, and that is fine. But insofar as he is trading off the welfare of his patient against the welfare of others, he simply cannot do that and remain in the advocacy role.

I see no reason why it has to be the clinician who places those limits, even granting, as Dr. Aaron has argued, that someone must place those limits. I think it is far better that the rest of us in society put the limits, the way we have done with our transplants, for example. That is a perfect example.

CHARLES L. SPRUNG: I run an intensive care unit and from my perspective a lot of the problems that have been discussed are related to a lack of knowledge on the public's part and a certain amount of uncertainty that physicians have making decisions early on. It would be much more helpful to the physician not to put the patient into the intensive care unit, to withhold rather than to get the patient into the intensive care unit. Once the patient is in the intensive care unit, I think most would agree, it is hard to withhold things, withdraw things. Those are not medical kinds of decisions but moral types of decisions that physicians have to make on a daily basis but don't feel very comfortable making.

We have had several patients, over the last few months, who have had living wills—a patient with AIDS and a seventy-five-year-old gentleman who was a quadriplegic. It is interesting that one makes out living wills. You are sort of in the perspective: "I am healthy and I want to live life, but I don't want to have to go through those things."

But when you are at the decisionmaking process in the intensive care unit—Should I pull out the tracheal tube and stop the respirator?—then all of a sudden your perspective starts to change. Then the question is: Do you want to stop living or not? Many times you may have that autonomous decision. What happens to the incompetent patient who comes into the emergency room without that kind of information? Usually when a patient comes in in that sort of situation, the physician, because of the uncertainty, is obligated to do things. I think, in general, it would be much more helpful if society as a whole were more aware of this situation to help the physician make those kinds of decisions before they got sucked into the kinds of problems we develop in the ICU.

VEATCH: With regard to the moral preference for withholding over withdrawing, let me simply summarize what I take to be the almost universal consensus in the moral literature. That is that the two are morally equal, that there is no moral difference between the two. The one exception is that there are some people who argue that it is morally preferable to withdraw rather than to withhold on the grounds that when you withdraw you know what the effect of the treatment is. If you withhold without ever trying the treatment, you never know for sure what the effect of the treatment will be.

WILLIS D. GRADISON, JR.

Federal Policy and Intensive Care

The decisions that have to be made about intensive care are far more likely to be made by people dealing with the issues day by day in individual institutions and medical practices around the country than by bureaucrats or by legislators. Yet the federal government must have a health policy. Ideally that policy should have a number of goals. Certainly the three most important are to control costs, provide access to health care, and ensure the quality of health care. Of course, today the three goals seem to be cost containment, cost containment, and cost containment. This creates a conflict because, at some point, insistence on any one of the three goals impinges on the other two, and trade-offs must be made.

The trade-offs raise a series of difficult ethical dilemmas. Access accorded to one group may diminish access for another. Broadening the availability of expensive high-technology care where funds are limited may have an adverse impact on primary care.

Politicians make choices in ways that will minimize, and if possible eliminate, any public perception that they are rationing care or diminishing its quality. For example, the executive branch, within discretion granted by Congress, is now attempting to decide whether the cost of heart transplants will be reimbursable under medicare. When public sentiment called for action, Congress stepped in and decided to ensure dialysis treatment for everyone in the final stage of renal disease.

However difficult such health policy choices may once have been— I think they have always been difficult—they are far tougher in a revenue-neutral world. Before the passage of the Gramm-Rudman-Hollings bill, which was aimed at reducing the federal budget deficit, the general notion was that if some immediate cause needed relief, Congress would appropriate more money or create a new program. There certainly was not a feeling that you had to take something away from another group or restrict an existing program in order to

37

finance the new one. Certainly that reality—if it ever existed—does not apply to the world in which we live today.

Spending on health care must compete with other public or private spending. Treatment competes with research, prevention with care, the old with the young. Vexing issues abound, and the present fiscal restraints intensify them. We have known, as economists, that we live in a world of scarce resources. But the decisionmaking process in Washington in recent decades has conveyed the idea to the general public that if something needs to be done, we will find the money for it.

Now, unfortunately, we have to make choices. These are issues that cannot be put aside. We have to consider how far costs can be reduced without having an adverse impact on quality. Does the present payment mechanism for hospitals—the federal government's diagnosis-related group (DRG) system of rates—provide a fair distribution of adequate care among patients of different hospitals? Does the DRG system require our hospitals and physicians to make decisions that are not in the best interest of their elderly patients? Does a fee-for-service system of reimbursement encourage overutilization of physicians' services and, if so, what are we going to do about it? Do health maintenance organizations (HMOs) and competitive medical plans (CMPs) with annual fees for care encourage underutilization? How is quality to be measured, and by whom?

Congress, of course, is not set up to anticipate problems like this. Basically, it is a responsive institution, as the Founding Fathers meant it to be. Members of Congress are subject to premature and involuntary retirement every two years; the nature of the job tends to focus our minds on short-term decisionmaking. Crises, real and imagined, which show up in the nightly news, tend to move us to action.

Nonetheless, the critical questions of access and quality are matters that continue to concern members of Congress. Two pieces of legislation having to do with health care are now before the Congress. One bill, having to do with access, has five elements: extension of employment-based health insurance to cover laid-off workers and their dependents; creation of subsidized health insurance pools to allow people without employment-based coverage to buy health insurance, regardless of their health status; a requirement that states either establish a mechanism to fund hospital charity care or develop a plan to provide health insurance to all uninsured residents; advantageous tax treatment to encourage the self-employed to offer health insurance to their employees (there is a real gap in coverage of this group); and development of methods to lower the cost of health insurance to small businesses. It is important to note, in talking about access, that 75 percent of all uninsured Americans are employed or are the dependents of employees. Thus the greatest hope for progress is in working through existing employer arrangements and trying to encourage employers who do not have health care plans for their employees to offer them.

The second bill, having to do with quality, appears to be getting more attention than the bill providing for access. The bill requires the Department of Health and Human Services to develop a legislative recommendation for refining the prospective payment system for hospitals. The object is to better account for variations in severity of illness and in the complexity of cases. That issue, I think, is the greatest uncorrected problem posed by the DRG system. But we do not have the data needed to suggest how the DRG system should be modified, and this bill calls for a study of the issue.

Among other, less important provisions, hospitals would be required, soon after a patient is admitted, to give a written statement of rights with regard to hospital and post-hospital care. This is pretty much being done now, without the law. Beneficiaries would have a right to appeal a denial to continue their hospital stay to the peer review organization (PRO). And hospital plans that offer physicians incentives for meeting targets that limit either lengths of stay or the case cost for individual patients would be prohibited. The bill also would require hospitals participating under medicare to set up criteria for discharging patients.

Governmental attitudes toward health care generally and intensive care for the elderly in particular will, I think, increasingly be marked by uncertainty toward the financing of care. This will be true not only in direct health issues, like medicare and medicaid and medical research, but also in the broader context of fiscal policy. Put more bluntly, federal dollars are soft dollars, and federal funding is likely to continue to be an uncertain.

Following the lead of the private sector, the federal government will try to become a more prudent buyer of health services, perhaps a downright stingy buyer if it utilizes its potential market clout.

Greater emphasis will be placed on HMOs and on annual per capita fees for care, thus reducing the federal role in defining the scope of services to be offered and leaving the measurement of quality to outside groups.

Congress is near the end of the road in legislating cuts in the health budget. But budget restraints may be exercised through regulatory rather than legislative action, with occasional expressions of congressional outrage, as in the reaction against the administration's plan to reimburse hospitals for capital expenditures under medicare. The squeeze will continue to be on providers, not on beneficiaries.

As federal funds for new programs become harder to find, the private sector will be required by law to carry the costs of activities that once were governmentally financed. Medicare, for example, is now the secondary payer for the working elderly. Employers who maintain a group health plan will have to provide an option for continued coverage of widows, divorced spouses, and spouses of employees eligible for medicare. And a similar concept has been proposed for coverage of the unemployed.

Financial stringency will heighten the awareness of ethical dilemmas and stimulate needed and valuable debate and analysis. I am a member of the newly appointed Biomedical Ethics Board, which has three Republicans and three Democrats from both the Senate and the House. We are not even organized. It is difficult to anticipate what our agenda will be. I think that it is significant that this group is being created as a follow-on to the President's Commission for the Study of Ethical Problems in Medicine and that members of Congress are becoming directly involved.

But in the end, members of Congress will be the last people in the country to have their fingerprints on any policy that even appears to deal with rationing of health care. Yes, we will allocate scarce resources, but we will not ration. We will leave that to the health care community.

Discussion

MICHAEL A. RIE: I wonder whether Mr. Gradison could tell us how the Congress would be prepared to assist us in addressing the dilemma expressed by at least two speakers that citizens have a right to health care and, in that right, have negligence entitlements under the common law which would allow them to bring litigation against us. It would seem to me that we have to have affirmative public disentitlement policies that would set aside those negligence entitlements.

Where do you see the American people's rights to bring legal actions for care which is outside our social policy, either institutionally or locally?

WILLIS D. GRADISON, JR.: One of the most perplexing parts of this, from a legislator's point of view, is the enormous variations in care and in judgments about what is appropriate care that exist within the medical profession. I hope that over time, as experience develops, it would be possible to have far greater consensus, not about just a single answer to a problem but greater consensus than exists today with regard to what is appropriate care. I hope there can be development of generally accepted protocols for the treatment of particular illnesses, which would provide not an absolute yes-or-no answer for the practitioner but something more to rely on than professional judgment which leaves one open to second-guessing through the legal process.

The entitlement which is provided under law—let's say for the elderly under medicare—does not speak to whether a particular case is entitled to transfer from the operating suite into the intensive care unit, or for how long, or even whether care should be provided by a specific institution or, after stabilizing, the patient appropriately can be transferred. I don't know any way to centralize decisions of this kind. Perhaps I have been missing something in reading Schwartz and Aaron's book, but my sense of it is that even in the British system, which seems to be highly centralized, there is some variation from area to area, depending on the availability of resources, in the decisions actually made about particular cases. And I would imagine that in our country that would continue to be the case. Our patients, as that book pointed out, tend to shop around. They don't take no for an answer. They are not limited to going to one doctor; they can go elsewhere if they can pay the bill.

So, I can't give you any explicit hope that the risks of legal liability will be waived by national legislation. I don't want to make it sound easy, but I hope that there would be a development of a greater sense of what care is appropriate in a particular situation than I sense exists today.

STANLEY L. LOFTNESS: I would like to have you comment about access—the quality of access to medical care for all citizens and whether or not there really is a societal demand that access to care and to the quality of care and types of care be equal for every citizen.

GRADISON: Well, first, access isn't equal now. Secondly, it is difficult to see how one could make it exactly equal, but I am sure that is what you are asking, and I am not trying to put words in your mouth.

I think a multi-tier system is almost inevitable in a society which has some degree of free enterprise. Even in Britain, private practice is starting to grow. For some reason, some people who can afford to go outside the existing system think it is worthwhile. So I guess even there a two-tier system is developing once again.

Certainly a society which calls itself compassionate and which has some sense of egalitarianism about it, as we do—and a society which does, in many ways, concern itself with outcome as much as with opportunity—has got to be for some semblance of equality of access. But what we are facing now is the extraordinary irony that access granted to certain groups in the community has made it harder politically to extend access to those not covered.

I served as assistant to the secretary of HEW thirty-odd years ago. I remember the early discussion of what became medicare. It was that that would be the foot in the door. First you would take care of the elderly, and then, having done that well and gotten popular support, it would be access and, more directly, federal financing would be extended to provide access for other groups.

I think that obviously hasn't happened and, indeed, that the success of employer-financed plans, plus medicare, has substantially diminished the public push to cover everyone else.

I seriously doubt that there is going to be any felt need, the sort of thing that moves congressmen to action, to extend these programs on a nationwide basis. I think it is going to be done a piece at a time. Maybe we can do something in the catastrophic area for various age groups and not just the elderly, but it is going to be a very slow and very expensive process. There are a lot of differences between the United States and Britain, and there are not a lot of ways to measure health care beyond mortality rates. But my reading of the numbers is that the British end up, at least with regard to mortality rates, with a result very similar to ours at a cost as a percentage of their gross domestic product of about maybe just over half of ours. But we are not going to scrap our system. We believe in entrepreneurial politicians, entrepreneurial physicians, entrepreneurial hospitals. Given that choice, I think it is going to be a matter of how we can marry that kind of a system with the needs, not changing the system entirely. I think we are past that. It is not even on the table.

WILLIAM A. KNAUS

Criteria for Admission to Intensive Care Units

The medical community needs precise criteria governing admission to and discharge from intensive care units (ICUs). We need explicit criteria to help us make decisions that have previously been left to the discretion of individual physicians. Persons involved in making local and national health policy should take an active part in developing these criteria.

THE COMPLEXITY OF DECISIONS

One of the major reasons that we need explicit criteria for admission to ICUs is the complexity of the decisons we must make. As Daniel Bell, the Harvard sociologist, has pointed out, we are now in the post-industrial portion of our history; theoretical discoveries are pushing back the frontiers of scientific knowledge and are being rapidly succeeded by direct practical applications. Nowhere is this more true than in the modern practice of medicine and the subspecialty of intensive care.

In less than three decades, we have gone from a practice in which the physician could place all of the diagnostic and therapeutic choices available to him in a small black leather bag and take them to the bedside of a critically ill patient to a practice that requires elaborate pharmaceutical and diagnostic support for the physician who tries to provide state-of-the-art care.

Doctors no longer go to the bedside of critically ill patients. Rather, patients are brought to intensive care units where teams of physicians and nurses use an array of complex devices to monitor and restore physiologic balance and thereby delay or, better, avoid death. The difference in the nature of medical work is readily apparent in the treatment of a patient with heart failure. In 1956, the physician sat

44

alone at the bedside examining the patient with his stethoscope and feeling his pulse. What he heard through the stethoscope and what he felt at the patient's wrist were the basis on which he used his intuitive judgment to determine the appropriateness of giving or withholding therapy—in this case digitalis, the only drug he had to stimulate a failing heart.

The patient in 1986 with heart failure is admitted to an intensive care unit. Immediately, a technician inserts a catheter into his radial artery, and the size and the shape of his pulse are promptly and publicly displayed above his bed. No need for any intuitive judgments; the facts are clear for all to see. Another catheter is introduced into his heart to measure the efficiency of cardiac performance and the adequacy of blood delivery to the rest of his body. In order to interpret these findings, the physician must have a detailed and precise understanding of complex and rapidly changing physiologic relationships between oxygen delivery, demand, and consumption. These calculations are too complex for direct intuitive judgment, so computers have been programmed to provide the answers. Once the computer data are in hand, the physician must choose treatments from a variety of drugs that stimulate or depress the heart, increase or decrease the body's peripheral resistance. The choice of each drug will, in turn, lead to changes in the cardiac variables, which will then have to be reevaluated. Much of this fine-tuning of therapy versus physiology requires precise practical and theoretical knowledge and all of it demands teamwork—but seldom stethoscopes.

The use of a limited number of highly personal, intuitive observations as the basis for therapy contrasts sharply with the integration and synthesis of large amounts of objective and theoretically derived data supplied by groups of individuals working toward a common therapeutic goal. The nature of medical work has changed dramatically. But the change concerns how the patient with heart failure is treated, not whether the person should be treated or how decisions should be made to stop or limit treatment.

To keep track of the data available on critically ill patients and ensure that essential things are done, many physicians and institutions have developed protocols and guidelines for the treatment of critically ill patients with various diagnoses. While many persons object to these changes as the arrival of cookbook medicine, there is a small but growing body of literature suggesting that the use of these guidelines improves patient care. If such guidelines are an important and growing aspect of decisions to treat critically ill patients, is it not appropriate to also consider them an essential adjunct for decisions to admit to and discharge from intensive care—decisions which, by their very nature, are more complex and far-reaching than the choice of a particular drug?

THE CONSEQUENCES OF THE DECISION

A decision not to undertake intensive care places the patient, the physician, and the institution at risk. For the patient, the decision to forgo intensive care could mean an increased risk of complications or even an increased risk of death. For the physicians, nurses, and institutions involved, such decisions can also create important ethical and legal risks.

The public nature of the decision is also an important consequence. Today, the decisions made in intensive care units are often recorded in the public press and frequently debated in courts of law. They also are made in the presence of and with the involvement of a wide variety of interested spectators, other physicians and nurses, along with family members and friends. The very public nature of these decisions requires that there be some public consensus regarding the decisions, and this is another reason to pursue the development of specific ICU admission criteria.

THE COST OF THE DECISION

The final consequence is the cost of the decision, but not only in terms of dollars. While it is clear that the dollar cost of medical care, especially intensive care, is large and growing, we are spending far more than money. Intensive care is a very intensive social activity. Proper care of the critically ill requires a large number of highly skilled physicians, nurses, and technicians working closely together to achieve common goals. These highly skilled and highly equipped teams work best when they are challenged with patients who require and can potentially benefit from their skills.

Like other highly skilled teams, professionals working in intensive care need to be given clear goals and objectives, and to be stimulated with new and honest challenges. If their skills are not used because there are frequent admissions of stable noncritically ill patients, their skills will atrophy and their attention to potentially important details will be reduced. On the other hand, an intensive care unit team will rapidly lose its spirit if it is frequently presented with terminally ill patients, for whom little more can be done than to prolong their dying and possibly even increase their suffering. Indeed, the phenomenon of burnout in critical care, I believe, is more related to asking physicians and nurses to do the inappropriate than to asking the impossible. These are the reasons underlying the need for precise criteria for admission to and discharge from intensive care units.

CHARACTERISTICS OF ADMISSION AND DISCHARGE CRITERIA

The overarching characteristic of any proposed admission or discharge criteria should be their explicit dependence on estimates of the probability of benefit from intensive care for the individual patient. With primary emphasis on probabilities, estimates from every direction will focus on the two major medical indications that intensive care patients should be given: the monitoring of those at risk of developing acute, life-threatening problems and the treatment of those with severe existing diseases. For patients admitted for monitoring, probability estimates will predict the chances of the patient's developing the feared complication; for patients who are critically ill, probability estimates will focus on the risk of death and the likelihood that intensive care treatment will lower that risk.

As the world of medical practice has become more complex and diverse, so has it become obvious that one patient's or one physician's claim to intensive care can no longer be absolute. Most such claims must now be considered in light of other competing patients' needs and in view of the new scarce resources, such as organ transplants, that our scientific progress has produced. Probability estimates that are based on objective, accurate, and reproducible estimates of risk, need, and potential benefit for intensive care allow us to begin to perform these comparisons in a democratic and scientifically rigorous manner. Though our ability to predict or prognosticate is still limited, even an imprecise measure of what we are really after—probability— is preferable to an exact measure of any other criteria—especially money and power.

Formal, objective estimates of the probability of benefit, however, are only one aspect of the information needed to draft and initiate criteria for admission to ICUs. We also need a more explicit public investigation and discussion of values, patient, professional, and public—the "tragic agonizing decisions" that have assumed theatric and dramatic connotations because they have not been openly discussed. We must acknowledge and incorporate into our criteria the fact that various individuals, faced with similar situations, will make different decisions. While all individuals value life, relative values change over a lifetime and they also vary according to the quality of life. For some persons, the combination of a low probability of benefit and a poor quality of life would be sufficient to forgo the opportunity provided by intensive care to prolong that existence. For others, that combination of factors would result in a decision for treatment. Admission criteria must make provision for this type of individual autonomy.

Neither patients nor physicians, however, can have unlimited freedom. Both must realize that demand for complex, sophisticated, expensive, and personnel-intensive medical care that today's medical system provides can never be absolute. The demand must be modulated by the probability of benefit, the resources currently available to provide it, and the competing demands of other individuals. Thus, while admission and discharge criteria will be rooted in probabilities, the thresholds for implementing them must be dynamic and adapted to changing circumstances.

This is where public accountability directly enters decisionmaking. Local, regional, and national leaders help develop and support standards for the provision of intensive care to which institutions and society can turn for guidance. Only through the provision of such explicit criteria can we ensure that considerations of social justice are taken into account.

How should we begin to make these adjustments in our medical system? An early step should be at the national level. We should sponsor and promote research aimed at finding better information on which to base our risk estimates. We need to make the science of prognosis and prediction an integral part of medical science, equivalent to diagnosis in its potential impact on patient care. We should develop a national commitment to prognostic research along the lines of the major units of the National Institutes of Health. This will provide the scientific visibility and support that will encourage young physicians to undertake scientific careers emphasizing prognosis and will move it into the mainstream of clinical practice.

Because prognostic information will never be perfect, these probabilistic estimates must be modified with human considerations and a strong sense of societal values. We have to ensure that, when there is substantial imprecision regarding the future, emphasis shifts to the rights of the individual. Even when there is a reasonable measure of certainty, we will also want to maintain sufficient flexibility for personal prerogatives and desires to be considered.

This will require strong leadership, from the people who pay for medical care and the people who deliver it, but especially from physicians. I see no way for our medical system to meet the new challenges unless physicians assume a new expanded responsibility for making decisions for the common good as well as for their individual patients. I also see no conflict for physicians—for in the vast majority of instances, what is in the best interest of the patient is also in the best interest of society. In those rare cases when resource constraints limit essential services, the physician should continue to look after the patient's best interest within the options available. To claim that the only way a physician can represent a patient is to have unlimited resources is both naive and, in my opinion, not responsive to the times in which we live. No matter how good our intentions, not everyone can have a heart transplant.

Such a shift will cause profound changes in our medical system. For most of this century we have concentrated on creating a medical system that uses the individual doctor–individual patient relationship as the major and often sole source of protection for scientific, moral, ethical, and societal values. Our reliance on individual judgments has served us well, creating a technically advanced and extraordinarily successful medical care system, the most advanced and most innovative in the history of medicine. Today, however, our very success threatens our future. Unless we can find a more precise, scientifically based method for the allocation and rationing of advanced expensive services like intensive care, we will be progressively forced to rely on economic criteria to decide who receives what services. This will surely lead to decreased public trust for the medical profession and, with the erosion of public support, increased injustice. This is my major reason for imposing a formal collective structure on a system that has, until now, been operated informally by and for individuals.

THE DEVELOPMENT OF INSTITUTIONAL ICU COMMITTEES

Institutional committees should be set up to review literature in prediction pertaining to criteria for admission to and discharge from intensive care units. These committees would develop criteria designed to meet the needs of their patient population. Such criteria would state the obvious but important fact that patients meeting brain death criteria would not be candidates for admission to continued treatment in an ICU unless they were potential organ donors. There would be little flexibility in these criteria, because the probability of a meaningful recovery has been well established as being vanishingly small. The committee might also decide that some less certain but extremely pessimistic clinical conditions (for example, advanced metastatic carcinoma or severe cirrhosis and acute respiratory failure) are not appropriate indications for ICU treatment. Restrictions on ICU admission for such patients, however, would be flexible enough to allow that, under very specific circumstances, a patient who met the criteria and would otherwise be denied intensive care could be admitted for a brief period of treatment if agreement could be reached beforehand on the time in which a response was expected.

The concept of a response to treatment distinguishes the criteria for admission to the ICU from the criteria for continued treatment. At our current state of knowledge and predictive ability, it is difficult to identify prior to treatment large numbers of patients for whom admission to intensive care is inappropriate. This should not be construed, however, as a statement that admission to an ICU is a necessary rite of passage for all critically ill patients. Rather, it is an acknowledgment of the current limits of our predictive knowledge and a sign of future challenges. The same challenge applies to the criterion for continued treatment; with the information obtained after we initiate intensive care, we can be more certain about the probability of benefit—precisely because we know whether the patient has responded or not to our initial efforts. In my view, this information makes it easier, not harder, to withdraw life support as opposed to withholding treatment.

Therefore, I would have the criteria include statements that patients who had failed to respond to initial treatment (for example, patients who had developed severe failure of several organs) should not be provided unlimited future treatment. I would then have the various categories (monitoring, active treatment, and so forth) assigned relative priorities so that triage decisions could be made.

Once the criteria were drafted, I would have them approved not only by the hospital's medical staff but also by the hospital's board of trustees and by other appropriate interested organizations, such as insurance companies. Public review and comment would ensure that the democratic, pluralistic nature of our society would be represented. This review would also provide time for public comment and revision and for discussion of how the criteria would be implemented. Initially the ICU director or his representative should be given responsibility for implementing the criteria. This person would have to be fully supported by the medical staff and hospital administration, especially when conflict arose. Such support would also be an important acknowledgment that the criteria represented collective judgment and not the opinion of any single individual.

ROBERT BAKER

Beyond Do-Not-Resuscitate Orders

Do-not-resuscitate (DNR) orders are exemplars and symbols of an emerging consensus of legal and medical policy on limitation of life-sustaining interventions. In this paper, I challenge this consensus by discussing the background of emergency decisionmaking and clinical "civil disobedience" that prompted the creation of these orders. I argue that, in part because of certain unanalyzed presumptions carried forward from this context, present DNR policy inverts the accepted notion of patient consent and biases intensive care practice in favor of therapeutically unwarranted aggressive interventions. I argue further that DNR policies ought to be replaced by a system of advance directives that will permit patients, or their surrogates, to give prior consent to cardiopulmonary resuscitation (CPR) and other intensive care interventions.

THE EVOLUTION OF DNR POLICY

On August 12, 1976, the *New England Journal of Medicine* featured articles discussing nonresuscitation policies at two Harvard teaching hospitals, Beth Israel and Massachusetts General.[1] The article describing Beth Israel's policies on discontinuation of treatment was entitled "Orders Not To Resuscitate" (ONTR). Once Beth Israel had written the unspeakable, the initials ONTR and DNR slowly percolated from patients' charts onto the pages of respectable medical journals. (In 1983, when the President's Commission for the Study of Ethical Problems in Medicine published a compendium of policy statements on discontinuation of treatment in intensive care units,

1. Mitchell T. Rabkin, Gerald Gillerman, and Nancy R. Rice, "Orders Not to Resuscitate," and Critical Care Committee of the Massachusetts General Hospital, "Optimum Care for Hopelessly Ill Patients," *New England Journal of Medicine*, vol. 295 (August 12, 1976), pp. 362–64 and 364–66.

the most common title given to the policies was DNR or do-not-resuscitate orders.)[2] Despite their hard-won respectability, these expressions and the nonresuscitation policies referred to as DNR protocols are essentially products of hospitals' clinical floors and the moral politics of the ward. They are thus preeminently practical documents designed to control and justify clinical practice.

The specific clinical practice these policies were designed to control was slow-coding. "Slow-coding," an expression in hospital-corridor argot, derives its sense from the expression "code"—which means an emergency, or a state (typically of a patient) that requires an emergency response. Thus, the expression "the patient is coding" means that the patient's physical condition requires an immediate, emergency response—typically, cardiopulmonary resuscitation. To slow-code is simply to respond to a code slowly enough to guarantee the ineffectiveness of the response—to stop for coffee and a doughnut, for example, while the patient is undergoing a cardiopulmonary arrest.

Why do clinicians slow-code? Consider the following case report published in the *British Medical Journal* in 1968:

> On the tenth day of the gasterectomy the [sixty-eight-year-old male cancer] patient [a retired physician] collapsed with classic manifestation of massive pulmonary embolism. Pulmonary embolectomy was successfully performed in the ward by a registrar [a physician]. When the patient had recovered sufficiently he expressed his appreciation of the good intentions and skill of his young colleague. At the same time he asked that if he had a further cardiovascular collapse no steps should be taken to prolong his life, for the pain of his cancer was now more than he would needlessly continue to endure. He himself wrote a note to this effect in his records, and the staff of the hospital knew his feelings.
>
> His wish notwithstanding, when the patient collapsed again, two weeks after the embolectomy—this time with acute myocardial infarction and cardiac arrest—he was revived by the hospital emergency resuscitation team. His heart stopped on four further

2. President's Commission for the Study of Ethical Problems in Medicine and Biomedical and Behavioral Research, *Deciding to Forego Life-Sustaining Treatment* (Government Printing Office, 1983).

occasions during that night and each time was restarted artificially. The body then recovered sufficiently to linger for three more weeks, but in a decerebrate state, punctuated by episodes of projectile vomiting accompanied by general convulsions. Intravenous nourishment was carefully combined with blood transfusion and measures necessary to maintain electrolyte and fluid balance. In addition, antibacterial and antifungal antibiotics were given as prophylaxis against infection, particularly pneumonia complicating the trachaeotomy that had been performed to ensure a clear airway. On the last day of the illness preparations were being made for the work of the failing respiratory center to be given over to an artificial respirator, but the heart finally stopped before this endeavor could be realized.[3]

The case of the dying physician typifies the interventional irrationality that precipitates slow-coding. Ultimately, the rationale of therapeutic interventions is to promote patient autonomy, that is, patients' ability to control their bodies and minds. Disease, injury, and disability erode, impede, or destroy autonomy; the purpose of therapeutic interventions is to forestall or to reverse this erosion. In the end, the ultimate objective of therapy is to support the ability of persons to control their own lives. In this case, however, an interventionist imperative subverted this objective. The patient had asserted his autonomy by explicitly requesting the cessation of further life-prolonging interventions. Yet treatment continued despite the fact that it offered no hope of cure and no release from pain and, just as important, was in defiance of the express wishes of the patient. Nonetheless clinicians, responding to an irrational therapeutic imperative, dutifully obeyed their orders.

Slow-coding arises when clinicians refuse to obey these imperatives; it is a state of clinical civil disobedience—that is, a situation in which clinicians refuse to obey an imperative for irrational or unconsented interventions, even though they are mandated either by doctors' orders or by hospital or unit policy. As in all cases of civil disobedience, it is justified by an appeal to a higher level of rationality, justice, or humaneness.

Civil disobedience, however noble, is an inappropriate premise

3. Reprinted in Jay Katz, *Experimentation with Human Beings* (New York: Russell Sage Foundation, 1972), pp. 709–14.

for institutional policy. It is unacceptable in the context of critical care medicine because it subverts fundamental structures of responsibility and accountability. The potential for error is far too great. Written medical records were invented to coordinate patient care over time and between clinicians, to assist in the development of rational treatment plans (based on accurate information), and to provide for medical review and accountability. Reverting to informal, unwritten understandings undermines the integrity of the decisionmaking process, maximizes the possibility of miscommunication, and potentiates irrational, even irresponsible, actions. So, as civil disobedience—that is, slow-coding—became more prevalent, responsible clinicians sought to control it by converting it into written "no-code" orders—orders not to call a code on a patient. Many intensive care units still use the expression no-code, or the initials DNR, or even more cryptic notations such as "blue star," or "OBP" ("on the banana peel," which, in hospital-corridor argot, means "slipping away" or dying) to indicate a do-not-resuscitate order.

Eventually these no-code procedures were formalized and written into manuals of hospital procedure as DNR protocols; they were also published in the medical literature and in reports of presidential commissions. A perusal of the published guidelines reveals certain universal features of DNR protocols. First, since these protocols attempt to integrate DNR decisions into standard medical practice, they require that do-not-resuscitate orders be treated like other medical orders. All DNR protocols stipulate that, after appropriate discussion and consultation, the responsible physician should enter a signed DNR order into the patient's medical record with a clear statement of the reasons for the order. Second, all DNR protocols restrict the class of patients for whom the order may be written to those whose probability of surviving hospitalization is believed to be nil or next to nil. Third, all protocols implicitly or explicitly recognize and accept brain death as an appropriate reason for withdrawing life support.

Although the broad outlines of a consensus about DNR orders exist, there is considerable disagreement about the details surrounding such orders. Protocols differ markedly on the range of patients considered appropriate for DNR orders. Some units consider any terminally ill patient to be an appropriate candidate for DNR; others restrict this designation to patients whose death is expected within hours. Protocols also differ on the degree to which patients and their families are to participate in decisions to limit therapy and on the role to be played by clinicians. Some protocols do not require patients or their surrogates to be informed that a DNR order has been written.

The protocols are further differentiated by the many exceedingly fine lines drawn to delineate the range of interventions considered appropriate for limitation. Some units exclude only cardiopulmonary resuscitation and, except for this exclusion, would treat the DNR patient "normally." Other protocols permit the restriction of all treatments—including ventilator support and nasogastric feeding. These restrictions are often parceled out in terms of categories—one category of patient might receive unrestricted care; a second might receive unrestricted care for short intervals (say, twenty-four hours) after which there will be a reconsideration of category status; a third might receive palliative care only (and, on some protocols, might have all nonpalliative care, including artificial ventilators, terminated or withdrawn).

Variations in DNR protocols and procedures often ignite intense, even heated, discussions in the medical literature. Yet the literature seldom remarks the more fundamental divergences in the conceptions of DNR presupposed by the various protocols—even though, from the perspective of moral theory, these distinctions are highly significant. All published DNR protocols seem to presuppose one of two fundamentally different conceptions of the nature of a DNR order. The dominant conception is that DNR protocols ratify the patient's right to consent to—and hence to refuse—treatment. Less common, but equally well known, is the conception of DNR protocols as a formalization of the clinician's therapeutic prerogative—the right to determine which therapies are appropriate to the treatment of a patient's conditions and to withdraw or to withhold ineffective, futile, or contratherapeutic treatments (including, in the case of a DNR order, CPR and other intensive care technologies).

Both types of protocol were published in the trail-blazing August 12, 1976, issue of the *New England Journal of Medicine*, although the paradigms are more clearly articulated in later protocols. The most commonly cited consent-DNR protocol was published by the Yale–New Haven Hospital. It states with exemplary clarity the underlying rationale of consent protocols: "The ultimate authority to determine the overall management objectives resides with the patient and/or the family....If a patient is conscious and competent, he or she has the clear right to refuse any treatment (including resuscitation) even if the consequences of such a refusal may be death."[4] The clearest statement of the rationale underlying therapeutic prerogative protocols is to be found in the Pittsburgh Presbyterian University Hospital's policy statement which proclaims that the reason for terminating treatment is to avoid "prolongation of death."[5]

Thus, although both types of protocol legitimate DNR orders, they do so on markedly different grounds. Consent-DNR protocols permit the termination of ineffective, contratherapeutic treatments solely on the grounds that the patient (or the patient's spokesperson) requests it. Therapeutic-prerogative protocols do so primarily on the grounds that the treatments are ineffective or futile or "prolong dying." Both types of protocol would have supported a decision not to resuscitate the physician dying of cancer in the case described above. On a therapeutic-prerogative protocol, however, the DNR order would have been justified by sheer futility of further treatment, whereas on a consent-DNR protocol the order would have been justified on the basis of the patient's request.

Consent-DNR protocols have come to predominate. They are the only type of protocol discussed or sanctioned by the President's Commission or the Hastings Center or by the public health laws of many states. The attraction of the consent-DNR protocol is not hard to fathom. Bioethics, at least in America, has tended to make the subject of patient autonomy (sometimes referred to as patient self-determination) its central concern and the informed and voluntary consent of patients the key issue in the clinical context. Anglo-American law respects and protects the right to consent—and, in part because of the legal sanctions surrounding the concept, so do hospital trustees. Families and patients can have few grievances against clinicians and hospitals, and little reason to have recourse to the law courts, when they themselves have consented to clinicians' actions. Small wonder then that in recent years a consensus of expert

4. Committee on Policy for DNR Decisions, Yale–New Haven Hospital, "Report on Do-Not-Resuscitate Decisions," *Connecticut Medicine*, vol. 47 (1983), pp. 477–83.
5. Ake Grenvik and others, "Cessation of Therapy in Terminal Illness and Brain Death," *Critical Care Medicine*, vol. 6 (1978), p. 285.

opinion has developed in which consent-DNR protocols have become the centerpiece of moral policy for critical care medicine.

THE PROBLEM WITH DNR PROTOCOLS

As should be evident from the title of this paper, my point is to challenge the consensus that has emerged around DNR protocols—including the currently favored consent-DNR policies. The DNR protocols did not emerge as the result of thoughtful policy decisions; they were developed as an institutional response to pressing problems of civil disobedience on the clinic floor. In essence, these protocols formalized and legitimated clinicians' civil disobedience, that is, slow-coding. To accomplish this, however, the DNR protocols paid a moral and logical price; they maintain the fundamental logic of the slow-code context—the aura of emergency in which it is reasonable to assume the appropriateness of unconsented resuscitation and other life-prolonging intensive care interventions. The presumption of favoring intervention permeates DNR protocols; it is understandable given the historical context out of which DNR protocols evolved, but it implicates all forms of DNR protocols into not one, but two fundamental errors: the fallacy of futile intervention and the fallacy of inverted consent.

As therapeutic-prerogative protocols recognize, there is no rationale, no medical justification, no moral justification for *futile* interventions. The mere fact that a patient, or the patient's family, wishes an intervention is not sufficient grounds for a clinician to maintain or initiate it. When clinicians believe that an intervention or treatment program will no longer serve its medical objective, they should so inform their patients or the patients' surrogates, and then alter or discontinue the treatment. Responsible clinicians do not have an obligation to maintain or initiate interventions they believe to be futile, and they certainly have no obligation to maintain these interventions to suit the medical theories of their patients, however heartfelt. They do, however, have an obligation to recognize that conceptions of futility may be value-laden, and to inform their patients, or their patients' surrogates, that they are considering a significant alteration of treatment plans, giving them the option of consulting other clinicians and of making alternative arrangements.

Unfortunately, the emergency context out of which therapeutic-prerogative protocols evolved tends to make them inhospitable to the patient's right to be consulted about these issues.

Consent-DNR protocols err in the other direction. They make ample allowance for the patient's right to consent, but trample the clinician's therapeutic prerogative by carrying forward presuppositions that are valid only in the context of an emergency. In an emergency, it is appropriate to administer CPR and other intensive care interventions without the consent of the patient. When carried forward into a nonemergency context, however, this presumption inverts the normal process of consent, requiring explicit formal consent only when nonintervention is contemplated. The natural result of this inversion is to create a bias toward intervention. "Doing everything"—continuing to administer CPR and other intensive care interventions—never requires anyone to face difficult prognostic questions. Nor need anyone arrange special, often painful, meetings with families and patients. Nor does it require special documentation. In the context of DNR orders, it is easier for everyone to continue to do "everything," including CPR, than to consider the possibility of limiting life-sustaining treatment.

Even if clinicians manage to overcome these procedural asymmetries and attempt to initiate DNR procedures, there is still a bias toward continuing aggressive interventions. For patients are often overwhelmed when their situation is explained to them. Families often have difficulty resolving their feelings of grief and guilt; many perceive requests for DNR as abandoning the patient. Ambivalence in such context is a natural, human response, and so intervention becomes hostage to hesitation. Under standard consent-DNR protocols, aggressive, costly, prognostically futile, and unconsented-to interventions continue by default.

In 1983, when the President's Commission published its recommendations favoring DNR protocols, there was little evidence of the ineffectiveness of DNR protocols in securing patient consent. Three significant studies of DNR practices issued since 1983 agree that even in hospitals with long-standing DNR orders, very few patients (between 14 and 28 percent) are actually consulted about DNR decisions.[6] This is true even on units that are careful to adhere to

6. Susanna E. Bedell and others, "Do-Not-Resuscitate Orders for Critically

DNR guidelines and that document DNR decisions. The built-in procedural bias toward continuing aggressive intervention combines with the aura of negativity and hopelessness surrounding DNR orders to incline clinicians to postpone discussing DNR with patients until they are so devastated by the dying process that the decision must be made by guilt-ridden relatives. The most significant of the three studies was conducted at Boston's Beth Israel Hospital. After noting that only 22 percent of all patients participated in the DNR decision, the authors concluded that "the DNR protocol's fundamental goal of allowing patients to participate in decisions about their own death has not been achieved."[7]

The President's Commission for the Study of Ethical Problems in Medicine has articulated a standard by which one can judge ethically sound medical decisionmaking:

> Good decisionmaking about life-sustaining treatments depends upon the same process of shared decisionmaking that should be a part of health care in general. The hallmark of an ethically sound process is always that it enables competent and informed patients to reach voluntary decisions about care.[8]

If judged by this standard, DNR protocols must be declared morally unsound; for, by inverting the consent process and by biasing decisionmaking toward aggressive interventions, the DNR process effectively deprives competent patients of the opportunity to reach voluntary decisions about their own care.

ADVANCE DIRECTIVES AND PRIOR CONSENT

In theory, most of the moral problems surrounding DNR orders could be resolved by normalizing the consent from the patient or a surrogate

---

Ill Patients in the Hospital"; Andrew L. Evans and Baruch A. Brody, "The Do-Not-Resuscitate Order in Teaching Hospitals"; and Jack E. Zimmerman and others, "The Use and Implications of Do Not Resuscitate Orders in Teaching Hospitals," *Journal of the American Medical Association*, vol. 256 (July 11, 1986), pp. 233–37; vol. 253 (April 19, 1985), pp. 2236–39; and vol. 255 (January 17, 1986), pp. 351–56.

7. Bedell and others, "Do-Not-Resuscitate Orders," p. 236.

8. President's Commission, *Deciding to Forego Life-Sustaining Treatment*, p. 89.

before a patient is admitted to intensive care units or administered CPR and other life-sustaining interventions—that is, by requiring consent for CPR and other intensive care interventions. In practice, this would involve significant changes in current policy and procedures. To obtain consent for CPR and other intensive care interventions in advance of emergencies it would be necessary to identify the populations at risk for such interventions. It would also be necessary to develop a procedure for explaining the nature of the interventions to these patients, for asking them to designate surrogate decision-makers, and for requesting that they give their consent, in the form of "advance directives," to such interventions in certain contingencies. To be effective, these advance directives would need to be requested not only of patients seeking admission to intensive care units, but of all cardiac patients, all patients scheduled for surgery, all nursing home patients, in fact all patients at risk for intensive care interventions, even outpatients.

Were there a system of advance directives for intensive interventions, intervention would no longer be a default option in nonemergency cases—it would be a decision consciously made either by the patient or by the patient's designated surrogate. Moreover, as the patient's prognosis changed, the contingent nature of the consent would continue to militate against decisionmaking by default. For the contingent nature of the consent given in an advance directive typically presupposes that the interventions in question are beneficial to the patient—that is, contingency consent is limited to interventions that clinicians believe to be beneficial. When these presuppositions are satisfied (that is, when the patient is in a physiological state where CPR and other intensive care interventions will benefit the patient), the clinician has a mandate for treatment. But when the presuppositions are not satisfied, there is no moral (or legal) mandate for treatment.

What this means, in practical terms, is that when clinicians find that further interventions are "futile" or confer "no benefit," the logic of contingency requires them to inform patients, or their surrogates, of this finding and to work out a new treatment plan. Most patients and surrogates, when informed that interventions are futile, will undoubtedly choose to seek further advice. Many will ultimately opt for a regimen of comfort and palliation, accompanied by cessation of life support—but they will not consent to continuing treatments declared "futile" by clinicians. Some patients, or their surrogates, will undoubtedly opt for continued aggressive intervention.

There seems to be a belief that these choices are morally equivalent. In my view, the continued aggressive intervention is morally problematic. For in an age in which intensive care interventions consume approximately 1 percent of the gross national product and in which cost consciousness has come close to enforcing rationing, any futile expenditure of medical resources is suspect. If medical resources deteriorate to the extent that allowing continued aggressive intervention would deprive potentially viable patients of intensive care, it may become necessary to bias the decisionmaking process against continued aggressive intervention—for example, by requiring that decisions to continue "futile" treatment be justified before a hospital ethics committee.

WOULD A SYSTEM OF ADVANCE DIRECTIVES BE PRACTICAL OR WISE?

Advance directives and various forms of contingency consent have well-established roles in cardiology, surgery, and other areas of medicine, but their widespread use on the scale envisioned here would constitute a significant policy change. Some clinicians might be hesitant, fearing the impact that such discussions might have on patients. Others may share the view, "Who wouldn't want to be resuscitated?" However, recent studies of patients who had suffered cardiac arrests and of outpatients who were potentially at risk for intensive care interventions indicate that many patients had thought about designating surrogate decisionmakers and about limiting life-sustaining intervention.[9] Almost all had wanted to discuss these subjects with their doctors, but in the study of CPR patients, only 19 percent of all patients had discussed CPR with their physicians before

9. Susanna E. Bedell and Thomas L. Delbanco, "Choices about Cardiopulmonary Resuscitation in the Hospital: When Do Physicians Talk with Patients?" *New England Journal of Medicine*, vol. 310 (April 26, 1984), pp. 1089–93.

their cardiac arrests.[10] They felt that their physicians had not encouraged discussion of those subjects. (These low rates held even when the physicians claimed to believe in discussing these matters with their patients.) Moreover, while physicians were able to recognize the wishes of patients who desired CPR, they almost invariably failed to recognize the wishes of those who did not desire CPR. The investigators found that patients who survived CPR, but who had not wished to be resuscitated, were neither demented nor depressed—and they still believed that they should not have been resuscitated when interviewed in a follow-up study six months later.

Perhaps the most important finding in these studies is that patients not only wish to discuss these matters with clinicians, they are capable of doing so.

> Most welcomed the opportunity to discuss their disease and functioning, as well as the complex familial and social factors that influenced their attitudes toward cardiopulmonary resuscitation. During our interviews, patients appeared able to set explicit limits on subjects they wished not to discuss. They also differentiated between the trauma of acute illness and the quality of life in general. Many seemed surprised at our questions and wondered how anyone could choose to forego a life-sustaining intervention. On the other hand, those who said that they would not be willing to undergo resuscitation were equally straightforward and assured in their responses.[11]

The system of advance directives proposed here would give all patients the opportunity of engaging in these discussions. They would have a real and meaningful opportunity to determine the nature of their medical care. Some patients may be emotionally and psychologically incapable of participating in such discussions, but to deprive the majority of patients of this opportunity merely to shelter the few patients incapable of assuming the responsibilities of self-determination would appear to be an unacceptable form of paternalism.

10. Bernard Lo, Gary A. McLeod, and Glenn Saika, "Patient Attitudes to Discussing Life-Sustaining Treatment," *Archives of Internal Medicine*, vol. 146 (August 1986), pp. 1613–15.

11. Bedell and Delbanco, "Choices," p. 1092.

LINDSAY ROBINSON

A Third-Party Perspective on Reimbursement Policy

Rationing is an issue that we have done our best to avoid talking about for too long. It is an issue that we will stumble over at great expense if we do not approach it deliberately.

While we in the insurance field have very little experience in setting a reimbursement policy to support rationing, it will be an easy thing for us to do. Currently, however, we are trying just about anything that seems to have some promise of forestalling rationing. When it becomes necessary to face the issue of rationing intensive care, it must be recognized as first and foremost an issue of social policy, not of reimbursement policy.

For those of us in the insurance field who spend time considering how to set reimbursement policy, there is one question from which all debates begin. To what degree do the policies we now enforce and the policy options we are considering provide incentives and disincentives consistent with public expectations and social policy? Consider for the moment that there are two parts to this question. The first simply states that it is the function of a reimbursement policy to provide incentives and disincentives. The second part implies that it is important to examine the nonfiscal jobs those incentives and disincentives perform.

In the 1940s and 1950s, when hospital-based medical care was viewed as a modern wonder to which all had a right, it was easy to set reimbursement policy. Given that there were too few doctors and too few hospitals, we simply provided incentives for the creation of new resources and for their use by physicians. In those days we considered how to develop a policy that would ensure adequate reimbursement for whatever seemed necessary to take care of an inestimable need for care. Those were the days when fee-for-service medicine and retrospective reimbursement of costs became institutionalized. These policies were providing incentives to do more of the modern miracles.

Today the issues we face are clearly more complex. Taking away existing resources or, even more difficult, going back on the promises we made to ourselves in the middle decades of this century is far more difficult than building on a new dream. This does not mean that the issues are to be analyzed differently, only that the analysis will be more complex.

To examine the jobs that incentives and disincentives perform, we have to determine what the social policy is, or at the very least what the public expectations are, that we are trying to design a policy to support. This is a determination we have to make each time we ask whether this or that approach is likely to work, whether diagnostic-related groups (DRGs) are doing the job they are supposed to do, or whether this or that consequence of a DRG system is good or fair. This is the question I hope we all spend the most time examining after this conference.

For an insurance company the public whose expectations we are first committed to satisfy is the purchaser of our policies. The purchaser may be a union, an employer, or a governmental agency. As these consumers have watched the rise in the percent of gross national product consumed by health care, the losses to the medicare trust fund, and the uncontrolled rate of increase in the cost of providing insurance benefits, they have called for the brakes to be applied to the cost escalator. Because they do not want to accomplish this by reducing existing levels of health benefits, cost containment has been their cry in the 1970s and 1980s—cost containment for the purpose of reducing the health care bill, not for the purpose of supporting rationing. Indeed, much of our activity in planning and cost containment could be viewed as an effort to reduce the bill enough to avoid rationing.

We have developed group care systems—health maintenance organizations (HMOs) and independent practice associations (IPAs)—to spread insurance risk to the physicians. We have developed prospective payment systems to spread risk to the institutions that provide care. And we have developed forms of copayment, deductible costs, and managed care programs to spread risk and responsibility to the individual and eliminate unnecessary care directly. For employers, we have developed tools for profiling health risks and utilization of benefits. We have taken part in experiments in health planning aimed at limiting the quantity of health resources and trying to regionalize or rationalize those that remain. We have developed more sophisticated data systems than were imaginable a decade ago.

A great deal of the literature prepared for this conference asks whether these techniques can do the job of eliminating waste and reducing cost. It explores the degree to which these policies are effective means of rationing. Let us look at the degree to which current reimbursement schemes support cost containment objectives. The techniques we are now employing do all they can to involve the individual, the physician, and the hospital in the economics of decisionmaking. The individual has been asked to take more out of his pocket than ever and to give up a measure of freedom of choice by enrolling in HMOs and plans offered by groups of physicians. The physician is under pressure from the hospital to avoid practice patterns that would cause peer review organizations (PROs) to deny government payments to the hospital. Physicians in HMOs are under pressure to keep costs down to protect both their referral base and their personal financial position in the health plan. Hospitals are under the pressures exerted by PROs to keep their practice patterns in line and by the DRG system to manage their profitable as well as their losing lines of business carefully.

In trade for asking these parties to play new roles and give up some of their insulation from rationing decisions, we have given very little as yet. We have offered individuals deeper coverage for health care in exchange for freedom of choice and the assumption of greater portions of the cost. We have offered physicians job security or an assured share of the market and incentive payments for conservative practice patterns in exchange for private practice where each sets his own fees. We have offered hospitals very little except the opportunity to make small marginal profits on those services where they can beat the norms.

There are clear signs that these policies slowed the runaway trends that, when projected, indicated that health would consume 100 percent of the gross national product early in the twenty-first century. There is still, however, a great deal of cost that can be cut.

More to the point in a discussion of rationing care for the critically ill are data on the use of intensive care units (ICUs) in New York State. The New York statistics are consistent with those in other studies. Between 25 percent and 30 percent of the amount spent on acute care is spent on patients whose stay in the hospital includes time in intensive care units. Of these stays 4 percent is for patients admitted for medical reasons who die within thirty days of admission. Of the remainder, as much as 25 percent is for medical patients whose illnesses could be termed of low severity. Eliminating these low risk–low benefit cases and those in which life expectancy is short could cut the bill for acute care by up to 6 percent overall.

While the policies of the past may not be adequate to address the problems we face today, the new policies now being tried will do quite well to help support proposed techniques for eliminating marginally beneficial use of the ICU. The DRG system provides powerful incentives to hospitals to examine their performance against national norms. Far more important, the system provides an analytical tool and a language that will allow physicians and administrators to discuss both the economic and the clinical relationship to the norm. This latter point has been very powerful in New Jersey, where hospitals and doctors have had years now to learn the language. Even so, they are just beginning to learn how to use it to identify the physician whose practice pattern causes revenue to be lost or to learn why one hospital is better than another in providing certain types of care.

When we add to this powerful language the tools represented by emerging schemes for classifying the severity of illness and methods for making prognoses, we will be far beyond the confusion and frustration these new programs represent today. I would even suggest that these tools, together with the ability to communicate in the DRG language, will allow us to evolve past using the DRGs for reimbursement and reserve them for this analytical function they were designed to meet.

To explore this possibility, we recently ran all the payments to the hospitals in New Jersey for the years 1982–84 through a computer to see what changes DRG pricing incentives might have brought about in the use of intensive care. We assumed, from the literature detailing how hospitals lose on cases that include ICU days, that there would be a decrease in the number of patients admitted to intensive care units and in the number of days spent there. To the contrary, the number of cases that included use of the ICU increased 1.7 percent over the two-year period, and the days by 2 percent. The ICU use per case had increased by 0.3 percent. Also of interest was the fact that use of the ICU for patients under sixty-five went down 3.3 percent, and for those over eighty it increased 11 percent. While it is difficult to draw sweeping conclusions from these data, we find New Jersey's hospitals have managed to maintain their level of occupancy, increase profits, and increase ICU utilization at the same time. This may mean that the predicted losses that are underwritten by a prospective payment system will not occur, that the program can be managed, or that losses are caused by factors that the prospective payment system does not incorporate.

With respect to physicians, we have seen very clearly the ability of the HMO and the IPA to reduce hospital admission rates by 50 percent or more. While the reinvestment made in primary care and preventative services has generally been equal to the reductions in hospital cost, it remains to be seen whether a healthier population will reduce the need for intensive care in the future. At the very least it has made physicians far more conscious of the cost of health care and the relative value of different investments.

Today, my staff in Albany is meeting with medical staff from Yale to discuss the possibility of testing an ambulatory-visit group (AVG) system. Ambulatory-visit groups—working like diagnosis-related groups—can be used to establish a reimbursement scheme for visits to physicians' offices and medical work performed there, and for treatment at surgery centers and hospitals' outpatient departments.

These tools will help us to better coordinate the incentives operating on the hospital and the physician. We hope that they will get us out of the situation we now face where a hospital is penalized for an unnecessary admission but the doctor who ordered it is not, or where the hospital loses $4,000 on every patient admitted to the intensive care unit who is classified in DRG category 123 while the physician who treats the patient receives extra pay.

With regard to the individual, the private insurance market is responding rapidly to the expectation that we can preserve a basic level of benefits and protection without making the cost of insurance unaffordable. We are doing this by asking the individual subscriber to give up varying degrees of freedom of choice, on the one hand, and to choose levels of deductible costs and of benefits—like an automobile policy—on the other.

Through all of these responses we are trying to spread the risk and responsibility as far and wide as we possibly can. We are doing this to make sure that all of the players in the decisionmaking process have a real stake in the game and some cards to play. We expect that the analytical tools provided by DRGs, AVGs, severity-of-illness indicators, prognosis measures, and other clinical and economic data will assist us in cutting costs. We hope they will help us in evaluating the difficult choices we will face when the resources available will not meet the legitimate need. At that point we will have to turn to social policy for guidance. We who try to set reimbursement policy to provide appropriate incentives and disincentives will need to know whether the objective is to ration to all equally or to ration according to ability to pay, whether the regionalization of services is to be continued or abandoned, whether the physician and the patient are to be protected from the decisionmaking or the decisionmakers. Any of these objectives can be easily met by the reimbursement specialist.

But these are not questions of reimbursement policy; they are questions of social policy. Reimbursement incentives should serve as a tool to implement social policy and never as a replacement for it. In fact, one of the lessons New York may well have taught us is that when the conviction required to articulate social policy openly is absent, reimbursement policy will prove a poor substitute. It will not be able to do a complete job with its measure of success or failure hidden from view, and it will fail to meet public expectation.

DANIEL TERES

Triage: An Everyday Occurrence in the Intensive Care Unit

As a practicing physician working in intensive care, I have become an "expert" in triage. My hospital, Baystate Medical Center in Springfield, Massachusetts, is a nine-hundred-and-fifty-bed community teaching hospital serving a population of half a million people.

Over the past twenty years the hospital has developed into a regional medical care center with programs in cancer therapy, chronic dialysis, cardiac surgery, cardiac angioplasty, trauma, and burn care. In addition, the hospital has a commitment to critical care medicine. We have set up our intensive care unit (ICU) as a flagship program with a house staff, interns, and residents from all services—medicine, surgery, anesthesia, obstetrics and gynecology, and medicine-pediatrics—rotating through one multidisciplinary ICU serving medical and surgical patients. Because it is the only ICU engaged in teaching—providing graduate medical education for interns and residents—in the region, the demand for beds in the unit has been tremendous.

When we say "demand," what does this mean? This usually refers to physician demand rather than patient demand. Physicians want their patients in this resident-covered ICU or in the teaching coronary care unit or adjacent cardiac surgery unit. These units offer supervision of residents by specialists in intensive care, a full range of consultants and special procedures, convenience, and the shared risk that protects doctors against legal liability. Consequently, over the past few years we have had more patients than available beds, more patients than our trained critical care nurses can handle, and often a waiting list of patients from neighboring community hospitals. Since the opening of our cardiac surgery unit ten years ago, we have never functioned at our licensed capacity because of an inability to attract and keep critical care trained nurses, a serious nationwide problem faced by virtually all ICUs.

For these reasons, I have become an "expert" in triage—in the microallocation of scarce resources. Civilian triage is not taught in medical schools, or in critical care fellowships. In many ways this is the antithesis of treating patients, since the emphasis is on deciding who will not be treated. In addition, triage is an onerous task which is guaranteed to bring its practitioner into conflict with his colleagues. It is also not a reimbursable function and takes the practitioner away from providing direct care or from teaching house staff or even from leading a sane existence.

Triage occurs to some extent in every hospital. At some institutions, it is the nursing supervisor who decides which patient gets the bed. In most teaching hospitals, it is the resident assigned to the unit who makes the decision. Since we have had this problem for several years, we have taken this responsibility away from residents and have delegated it to the intensive care physicians.

The triage officer has a variety of problems to deal with. There are patients who come to the intensive care unit from the emergency room, the operating room, and the general wards, and from other hospitals' ICUs. Patients undergoing high-risk, elective surgery (such as resection of an abdominal aortic aneurysm) are scheduled in advance for the ICU. But emergency operations and unexpected complications also occur in the operating room. There are only limited controls that an ICU's triage officer can place on the operating room, such as limiting the number of high-risk elective cases done per day, canceling elective surgery, or closing the emergency room.

How can the triage officer move patients out of the ICU? One way is to bypass the ICU altogether. We have developed intermediate care units that monitor patients' progress so that they do not have to go into the ICU. The Commonwealth of Massachusetts does not recognize the existence of intermediate care units because they are presumed to increase the capacity of acute care beds and are presumed to contribute to a further rise in the cost of care. My hospital has developed a limited capacity in intermediate care as a way of buffering the excess and periodic variability in patient demand and to help intensive care services. However, intermediate care is offered at regular room rates and with only a marginal increase in staffing.

The well-known *Von Stetina* case, involving triage, dealt with a hospital's failure to make space in its ICU for a patient. I predict that the next major lawsuit involving triage will be related to excess triage.

Several months ago, I received a letter from a lawyer, advising me that "in the event Mr. S. is removed from the ICU Section or from the support systems without the written consent of both Dr. S. and Mrs. P., my client has authorized me to proceed as vigorously as the law will require to compensate Mr. S.'s family for any and all damages which result from your actions." The twenty-year-old patient had been involved in a head-on collision with an oak tree, after which he developed severe brain and brain stem injuries. He had been in the intensive care unit for twelve days, was still on a respirator, and was doing poorly.

My associate was faced with a typical crisis one evening when ICU beds were filling. There were more patients than the staff could care for. My associate suggested to the family that the patient might be transferred to the neurosurgical unit, where he would be placed near the nursing station, with nursing, respiratory therapy, and his physician's services coordinated. There was no suggestion of withdrawing the patient from the respirator or of stopping treatment. However, there was a discussion about what the patient's "code status" was.

My response to the lawyer's letter was to ask him to act as a family adviser. The family had had considerable difficulty coming to grips with this patient's condition. They had been so distraught and disorganized that a younger brother had tried to assume overall responsibility. Two days after I received the letter, the patient had improved enough that he was able to breathe without a mechanical ventilator. He was safely transferred, under normal procedures, to a neurosurgical unit and several weeks after that to a rehabilitation unit where he has made a substantial recovery.

It is important to point out the distinction between civilian and military triage. In typical clinical practice, when a choice must be made between a patient who is recovering or improving from a critical illness and a patient who is on various kinds of life-sustaining equipment, has multiorgan failure and poor salvageability, and for whom no decision has yet been made to stop or withdraw treatment, it is quite clear which patient will be removed first from intensive care services. General nursing units are not able to accept the time-consuming, deteriorating ICU patients who are on mechanical ventilators and receiving infusions to support their blood pressure (unless the patient's chart shows that care is supportive and the patient is in a category of "do not resuscitate"). The opposite occurs in military triage; the patient who has a reasonable chance for recovery is given preferred status.

I can assure you that as hospital resources are reduced in the United States, civilian triage will become a common event. When I started my career in 1974, the intensive care unit at my hospital was just getting off the ground. In that year, the ICU clocked twenty thousand hours for patients on mechanical ventilators (a measure of work performed that we are required to report to the Joint Commission on the Accreditation of Hospitals). Until 1982, when we merged with a second hospital and started a cardiac surgery program, we were able to match patient demands with our resources. Today, we are recognized as a tertiary care center and a trauma center, and both the number of patients and the number who are severely ill have increased dramatically. We now clock thirty-five thousand hours annually for patients on *general wards* on respirators.

What is the appropriate workload for a given hospital or region? Does the number of ventilator hours that our hospital clocks represent excess care? Does it represent a failure to make decisions? (Before 1970 many trauma victims did not reach the hospital and patients requiring specialized, high-risk surgery went to Boston or Albany.)

I would like to suggest that these numbers represent, in part, the routine miracles of high-technology care that are performed each day throughout the United States. (In 1969 many operative procedures were not offered for elective surgery that are now available because of advances in intensive care medicine and in anesthesiology.) The increase in workload can also be explained, in part, by the prolonged care given to patients who do not recover promptly from a catastrophic insult. These situations require difficult ethical discussions about code status and limitation of care with the family if a patient's condition is deemed irreversible.

As a first step, we need to describe to the public what is happening to patients who wind up on prolonged respiratory support. Some of these patients are slowly dying of failure of several organs, others of failure of a single organ. Some may make a slow recovery over many months, but many will die (certainly a cruel fate). The net effect is a large number of patients who are chronically critically ill.

The next step is to express explicit policies to define which patients need intensive care, what the criteria are for discharge, and what steps are to be taken when triage becomes necessary. At Baystate Medical Center, ICU rules require that before we consider triage, we must first speed up the usual discharge procedure. That means examining the gray zone in which a patient meets medical and nursing criteria for discharge from an ICU but is not quite ready for admission to a general ward. We next tighten up our admission standards and take sicker patients who require invasive treatment. Patients who generally would be admitted for close monitoring or conventional therapy are kept on general wards or in intermediate care units.

An article in the *New England Journal of Medicine* examines a period of acute shortage of nurses in an ICU that combines coronary care and medical patients at the Massachusetts General Hospital. It shows that physicians were able to adjust their admission and discharge patterns so that no adverse effects occurred during this acute short-age.[1] Another article, in the *Journal of the American Medical Association*, describes triage as a common occurrence in a university hospital. It shows that when beds were tight, physicians could balance admissions and discharges and provide a high quality of care for appropriate patients.[2] What neither article describes is the pain and suffering that these heightened decisions cause. Take the example of a patient who has had surgery canceled because a bed was not available in the ICU on the day of surgery. The patient is prepared for surgery and at the last minute the anesthesia is withheld and the patient is sent home to await a new booking for the elective procedure. Obviously, this may be necessary on rare occasions. However, it is not in the best interest of patients (or the hospital and surgical staff) to do this often.

At Baystate, the final step when ICU beds are limited is the "triage mode." The rules read:

—Review estimated prognosis for each patient
—Cut back on invasive monitoring
—Cancel elective surgery

1. Daniel E. Singer and others, "Rationing Intensive Care—Physician Responses to a Resource Shortage," *New England Journal of Medicine*, vol. 309 (November 10, 1983), pp. 1155–60.

2. Michael J. Strauss and others, "Rationing of Intensive Care Unit Services: An Everyday Occurrence," *Journal of the American Medical Association*, vol. 255 (March 7, 1986), pp. 1143–46.

—Arrange alternative treatment site for patients who have not
responded to intensive therapy

—Contact area ICUs for transfer capability

We first review the prognosis of each patient, using clinical judgment.
We gnash our teeth and wring our hands and try to come up with
the best clinical estimate we can. In some cases we cut back on
invasive care so that we can spread nurses out to cover more patients.
At night we may limit the monitoring of vital signs and stretch the
assignment of nurses to two patients. At many hospitals, the standard
of care in an ICU has changed and nurses instead of covering one
or two patients may take care of three.

It is important that the public be aware of the ethical and medical
dilemmas that we face every day. If physicians are to make the
difficult decisions, we need to train them to function as knowledgeable
and fair triage officers in this new environment. Physicians who have
this responsibility should have a good working knowledge of medical
ethics, particularly regarding withdrawal of life support. The hospital
should have explicit policies regarding limitation of care and do-not-
resuscitate (DNR) or no-code status. And those policies should have
the support of the medical staff as well as the board of trustees.

We must study managerial strategies to learn how best to use
human and technological resources during routine periods (how to
regulate or schedule the flow of patients having elective surgery) as
well as during peak work periods marked by many emergency
admissions.

We must also make the public aware that a patient's autonomous
rights should be respected and encourage patients to identify loved
ones who will help make decisions for them if they become incapa-
citated. But how do we balance community interests against a family
that wants all care continued despite overwhelming odds?

And, we need to do more about research regarding triage. We
need to continue the support for research being done with prognostic
models. Such studies may be helpful in defining which patients
should be admitted to an ICU and which categories of patient should
have only a brief exposure to an ICU. The Society of Critical Care
Medicine (along with other professional medical societies) should
take the lead in presenting these issues to the public.

BARBARA R. GRUMET

Legal Perspectives on the Allocation of Intensive Care Services

Two major issues in the allocation of intensive care resources are entitlement and expectancy. Entitlement refers to the popular misconception that patients have a right to health care. There is no such thing as a right to any specific intervention, no matter what the patient says, or how insistent the family may become.

However, there are certain modifications to that statement. For example, statutes or regulations in a number of states say that certain kinds of patients may have a right to at least the beginnings of certain kinds of care, and, unfortunately, from the standpoint of providers of intensive care, some intensive care services may fall into this category. These laws say that patients who come to an emergency room with an allegation of a need for emergency treatment must be evaluated, and if their allegation is correct from a medical standpoint, they have to be treated. In states without such laws, courts have created this entitlement. Patients who have been turned away at the hospital door because they failed the "wallet biopsy," or because they needed care at 2:00 A.M. and all the physicians were at home sleeping, have sued hospitals for failure to provide needed emergency or intensive care services. The hospitals run into trouble in such situations because they are violating their obligation to provide needed medical services to patients in the community they are supposedly serving.

Medicare and medicaid patients are entitled to funding for certain types of services. What that means varies considerably. In some states, for example, medicaid patients are entitled to a maximum of fourteen days of hospital care. The diagnosis-related group (DRG) system that dictates payment rates for medicare patients presumes that a typical patient can be successfully treated within a specified time. In both situations, the fact that the time limit has expired cannot be used as a justification for discharging a patient who still requires hospital care.

Patients are also entitled to care at public expense if the care is "medically necessary." They are so entitled because the treating physician and frequently a third party such as a peer review organization (PRO) have determined that the care is medically indicated. That, presumably, means that the patient is going to receive some kind of benefit from the intervention.

Other so-called entitlements say that a provider cannot discriminate against a patient on the basis of factors such as race, handicapping condition, and, increasingly, ability to pay, or source of payment, or type of illness.

From a legal standpoint, the decision whether or not to admit a patient to an intensive care unit should be made in the same way that any other decision about medical care is made. Presumably, the medical decisionmaking is done by the physician who is deciding a course of treatment and is making the decision based on his or her knowledge, skill, and experience and on the standards of the profession. It is very important to remember that such standards are peer-driven. If there is no standard within the profession, the court will step into the vacuum and impose a standard. The court's determination may very well end up being the plaintiff's version of the need for services.

The second area to consider is the question of expectancy. Patients, their families, and the general public have come to expect certain types of care, certain kinds of outcomes from the medical experts to whom they turn for help. One very common expectancy is that almost any hospital of any size has intensive care services. About 95 percent of the hospitals in the United States with one hundred beds or more have what they call intensive care units. Another expectancy is that any hospital is going to have an emergency room.

However, there is a considerable amount of variation in the reality of services available. An intensive care unit can range from a highly specialized, highly technologically oriented unit fully staffed around the clock with state-of-the-art-trained care givers, to a partially staffed, minimally equipped unit with unclear lines of responsibility and authority.

This is one area where the difference between patient expectancy and hospital reality can cause legal complications. For example, I do not think it is a coincidence that virtually all of the horrendous malpractice cases involving injury to patients in emergency or intensive care situations occurred in so-called off hours. As an example, in the infamous *Darling* case of twenty years ago, a young man lost his leg because the general practitioner who had not set a bone since his days in medical school was negligent.[1] The hospital said, "This injury is not our fault; the physician is not our employee." The court said, "You are responsible because the public expects that when they come to you in need of emergency care you will have appropriately qualified caregivers and facilities available." This young man went to the hospital on a Saturday afternoon. The young woman in the *Von Stetina* case was denied admission to an intensive care unit at two in the morning.[2]

From an administrative and professional standpoint, this is probably one of the first areas where action could be taken to prevent problems. It is axiomatic that medical emergencies do not occur during normal business hours. Hospitals have to begin to recognize this and make accommodations to the need for around-the-clock staffing, or at least make staff readily available. You are collecting $1,000 a day, sometimes more, from reimbursers for providing highly skilled, highly sophisticated, life-saving intensive care. If you do not have the people there to do this, you should not be in the business of calling yourselves capable of providing such services.

Another expectancy is that if a patient needs an intensive care bed, it will be available. Standards from within the profession itself can go a long way toward easing what seems to be a chronic shortage of intensive care beds in some areas. One of the points that seems to be emerging from the literature is that there are some patients in some ICUs around the country who do not belong there. If these inappropriately placed patients fill the unit, what happens if a patient who really needs these services comes along? What happens if the family turn around and sue because they allege that the reason for their relative's death is the failure to provide needed intensive care services?

1. *Darling* v. *Charleston Community Memorial Hospital,* 33 Ill. 2d 326, 211 NE 2d 253 (1965).
2. *Von Stetina* v. *Florida Medical Center,* 2 Fla. Supp. 2d (Fla. 17 Cir. 1972), 436 Su. Rptr. 2d 1022 (1983), 10 *Florida Law Weekly,* 286 (Fla. May 24, 1985).

In this situation, the hospital that cannot justify a denial of needed services will be liable. Likewise, if the hospital has an open-door policy and cannot provide services because the unit is overcrowded and understaffed, it will be liable. If your unit is over capacity almost every day and you are saying, "We could not accommodate this patient because we did not have enough resources," that is very different from saying, "This was the only time in six months that we were over capacity, because we have a very responsible system for deciding who should benefit from these services, and we have used these procedures."

In other words, if a hospital has criteria for admission, retention, and discharge of patients in intensive care settings, those criteria can help justify decisions to provide, or deny, these services. The policies must, of course, be consistently applied, adhered to by the entire staff, and supported by the administration. Otherwise, they will not be worth the time and effort required to develop them.

Another dimension of the expectancy factor is that patients may expect the services to be available without having any idea of what intensive care services are, or what they can do for them. A lot of education is necessary, so that patients and their families have a realistic view of the advantages, and limitations, of intensive care. Many of the agonizing decisions that are made could be somewhat easier if the patient and family were let in on the process. I think that a little less paternalism and a little more partnership would make some of these decisions less difficult. In addition, more realistic discussions about the benefits and risks of intensive care would generate more realistic expectations on the part of patients and families.

Patients may or may not be entitled to intensive care services. They expect availability, quality, and a successful outcome. If there is a discrepancy between expectations and reality, legal complications may follow the medical complications. Professional standards for admission, retention, and discharge of patients can lessen problems of access to services. Hospital policies for proper staffing at all times will help alleviate problems of quality. And more education of the public, and communication between provider, patient, and family, will relieve the problems of unrealistic expectations about outcome.

Leadership in these areas should come from those in the best position to define standards: the providers of intensive care services.

Discussion

VALERIE RINKLE: I would like to know if some of the resistance to developing specific admissions criteria for ICUs is because of the possibilities that third-party payers may pick it up as the utilization-review-reimbursement type control. What is the likelihood that that will occur if admissions criteria start to proliferate?

WILLIAM A. KNAUS: I have not heard that as an objection to establishing explicit criteria. My personal experience has been that people who pay for medical care are running away faster from this question than even Congress is running away. So, I think that the likelihood that reimbursement would lead this discussion is extraordinarily unlikely. More likely, reimbursement is just going to follow and perhaps provide some obstacles. I don't see the insurance companies as a major player in these admission or discharge questions.

CHARLES L. SPRUNG: I have been told by the chief of staff of my hospital that I am a money-losing proposition. I agree with him. If we look at Dr. Rie's information about where we are spending a lot of our dollars, we are spending it on a lot of people who are going through the dying process. I think that will continue.

I also agree with him about things getting worse. Someone is going to figure that out and realize that we are a money-losing proposition and, therefore, physicians will be in a worse moral dilemma on a day-to-day basis for the kinds of decisions that will occur.

KNAUS: I want to respond to the point about the ICU being a cost loser. It is really symbolic we have this system. If any of you have traveled in other countries, the way that we relate medical care to dollars in this country is really very unique. Other countries don't do that. They don't talk about high-cost patients or high-cost services. They talk about the need to do certain things for people who need those services. One of the bad things about the DRG system is that it exacerbates the linkage of dollar amounts to individual patients. Not only do you now come in with an insurance card; you come into a hospital with a price tag. That is perverse. That isn't the way we should be making allocation decisions on a micro or macro level.

The ICU should not be viewed as a cost loser or a cost gainer to an institution. The question should be: "How big an ICU do we need to provide the benefit for the kinds of patients that we have in our hospital?" Not all the patients but all the patients who can potentially benefit.

What we have done with that is to create this perverse economic incentive to do certain things which don't make medical sense.

MICHAEL A. RIE

Professional Ethics and Political Power

For an intensive care physician examining professional ethics and political power, the burden is to find a way to function at the crossroads demarcated by individual patient care, on the one hand, and public policy regarding allocation of resources, on the other. We have heard evidence that intensive care medicine is very costly and consumes a disproportionate share, per patient, of hospital resources in a society whose health care resources are finite. This conference has avoided the dual issues of when and how our society creates a public allocation policy. We should be addressing the interplay between individual patient care and the alleged autonomous right to health care, on the one hand, and the circumscribing of that right by the policy of allocating communal resources, on the other.

Many of the participants spoke directly about health insurance issues, and it behooves us to note the differences between the public notion of health, home, and automobile insurance schemes. In the United States we are unable to decipher what it is that we are purchasing with health insurance dollars. When we purchase car insurance, we have a very clear idea of what we buy. We know what portion of costs is deductible and how much the out-of-pocket coinsurance expenses are. We know what the defined benefits are as the product is monetarized. If we choose to purchase cheap insurance that inadequately insures the value of our automobile or our home, then we are truly unfortunate when our house burns down and its value is only partially covered. However, no one has a notion that that is an unfair circumstance. There is no sense that one can go to a court of law or legislative body and claim that one is entitled to compensation for one's home having been burned down after one has freely elected to purchase an inadequate home insurance policy.

This type of analysis seems to escape us individually and as a society when we attempt to set up health insurance schemes. In health insurance we fail to specify the policy limits; they are typically left in vague terms. It is usually to the great advantage of bulk purchasers of insurance—government, large employers, unions—to leave contracts vague so as not to offend the consumer beneficiaries who are not the purchasing party.

Those of us who practice intensive care medicine find increasingly that the nature of our practice is intruded upon by our lack of resources and the vagueness of the health care policies under which patients come to us for care. Dr. Knaus spoke of the need for explicit allocation policies to define the patient's entitlements under intensive care. His was a communal plea from those of us who run intensive care units (ICUs) to establish a dialogue between the ICU staffs who act as allocators of health care resources and the governments and business purchasers that create policies defining the resources that will be dispersed in intensive care activities.

Our need for explicit guidelines and policies is a product of our litigious society which accords individuals incredible freedom but does not define their right to consume health insurance resources for marginal benefits from intensive care—particularly when the resources come from a system that draws payments for health care from a variety of sources. The ICUs in which we labor are not strictly created by Blue Cross, medicare, commercial insurers, health maintenance organizations, or medicaid. They exist by virtue of all health funding sources that feed into the overall hospital and physician budget.

I was more than dismayed but not surprised to hear Congressman Gradison say that "politicians make choices in ways that will minimize, and if possible eliminate, any public perception that they are rationing care or diminishing its quality." The perceptions of the Congress are not very different from those of the Business Roundtable or any corporate purchaser of health care. These general positions of the major creators of health policy are not compatible with the smooth running of intensive care units in the United States, particularly if one realizes that the number of ICUs and the number of hospitals are scheduled to shrink in the coming years.

We in intensive care medicine are increasingly faced with issues of patients' rights to consumption squeezing us from one side and cost containment and decreased resources squeezing us from the other. It is apparent that our society will have to create a new political role for us as patient advocates at the social level in our health care system. While it is not our duty to create the moral values that determine who will live and who will die, it clearly is our duty, as outlined by Dr. Knaus, to provide hard scientific data in the form of prognosis research on which to base public dialogue. It will not be sufficient to inform the Congress and to inform business purchasers. It will as well be necessary to widely disseminate this information through the public media so as to effect a widespread public health education program (parallel to the AIDS education effort) on the issue of intensive care expenditures, results, and choices.

The results of public education will undoubtedly lead to a second level of discussion between the direct beneficiaries of health care and the third-party purchasers of health care in which the health professions will act as informed advisers. As these dialogues are established, we may also anticipate further discussion about government attempting to shift costs to the private sector and about the intergenerational competition for resources from the medicare program which indiscriminately consumes the resources of a somewhat attenuated working population protected by private health insurance. As the private sector becomes more adept at insulating its contracts covering health care from the federal government's efforts to shift the cost of intensive care, we may anticipate that all parties (including state governments) will feel a greater need to negotiate a settlement in intensive care policy.

The end reality of this discussion is defining a just and reasonable system for allocating expenditures on and entitlements to intensive care. We are a pluralist society that holds different values about the worth of life in coma, the worth of life in old age, the worth of life in chronic infirmity, and the worth of life in robust youth. It is apparent that we must have a common procedural language of expression in public policy that would permit us to negotiate our differences in areas where we are obliged to assign monetary values to life in order to avoid widespread chaos in the public delivery of medical services. The cost of not negotiating our differences is to have an erratic allocation system (as we have now), in which healthy and viable individuals may die or suffer severe injury when they could have been saved and restored to good health while our resources go to those who are less likely to benefit from the resources because of a poor medical prognosis.

Tristram Engelhardt and I have recently summarized these issues.[1] We argue that the moral issues encompassed in assigning priorities in the allocation of ICU resources should be thought of as the public creation of an ICU entitlement index. The index is equal to *PQL/C*, where *P* is the probability of a successful outcome, *Q* the quality of success, *L* the length of life remaining to a patient, and *C* the costs required to achieve the therapeutic success. Each element of the index will be furiously fought over by the various interested parties. But the index is the only method that we can conceptualize that will allow for the existence of an intensive care system not based on force, not based on funding from a single source as in socialist countries, and allowing vastly conflicting moral communities to come together and negotiate freely a health care system in which they may have some common procedural interest in receiving integrated intensive care services.

Such an index will cause Christianity, Judaism, and other value-creating organizations to reexamine the foundations of the relative values they assign to health care and other primary social goals. Indeed, intensive care medicine and high-technology medicine in the latter twentieth century are the equivalent of Martin Luther and the Reformation for Christianity in centuries past. They challenge again and in a different historical way the major ethical standards on which the value creators in our society face the modern world. If Christians and Jews wish to have treatment for hypoxemia and shock, they must be prepared to define the limits to which half-way health care technologies should be expended upon the faithful in circumstances of marginal benefit. These are prerequisites if the organized religions are to be responsible members of a secular, pluralist, peace-loving democracy.

Perhaps the most intellectually contentious issue raised by the rationing of intensive care is the degree to which it challenges the major value-creating organizations in our society to decide how much they wish to participate in a pluralist democracy and how much they wish to pay privately for more care at marginal benefit than that which most mortals are willing to allocate. Although this conference

---

1. H. Tristram Engelhardt and Michael A. Rie, "Intensive Care Units' Scarce Resources, and Conflicting Principles of Justice," *Journal of the American Medical Association*, vol. 255 (March 7, 1986), p. 1162.

does not directly deal with religious values, I believe that these issues and their appreciation by those involved are as important to the creation of coherent intensive care policies in our country as all of the technical and specific issues addressed at this conference.

The cultural authority and the political power of intensive care professionals lie in their technical understanding of what technology can and cannot do for the universe of critically ill patients and in communicating such knowledge to all Americans. The intensive care community must be prepared to discuss honestly the economic consequences of failing to put monetary values on human life at the margin that can serve as a policy of nonentitlement for publicly agreed on categories of patients. Otherwise we shall continue to be perceived as chaotic and unjust health care professionals who were silent as the standard of care deteriorated. The spread of AIDS may now challenge our youth-oriented culture to confront the monetary consequences of epidemic young death competing for ICU resources with the chronic epidemic of expensive, biologically mandated death at the end of the human life span.

ROBERT BAKER, I. ALAN FEIN,
MARTIN A. STROSBERG & MAX HARRY WEIL

Caring for the Critically Ill: Proposals for Reform

Despite the diversity of perspectives represented at the conference on the rationing of medical care for the critically ill, there was general recognition that either clinicians themselves must control the rising costs of medical care or the federal government's preoccupation with cost control will create a system of de facto rationing. After the conference, we developed a set of proposals for the reform of intensive care practice to serve as a springboard and incentive for further discussion of this vital issue. At best, our proposals may lead to changes that will forestall, or perhaps even preempt, the need to introduce explicit rationing into the practice of intensive care medicine.

TIGHTENING ADMISSION STANDARDS

The inefficiencies of intensive care medicine are in large measure a result of the rapid growth of technology. Until recently, intensive care medicine, and life-support technology in particular, was regarded as experimental. Since the benefits of admission to intensive care facilities were not well documented, physicians were inclined to give almost all critically ill patients the potential benefit of admission to a special care unit.

As a consequence, admission to the intensive care unit became an expensive, and often agonizing, preliminary to death—a rite of passage notable more for its rituals than its rationality. Now that the outcomes of intensive care interventions have been more adequately documented, the futility of many of these admissions can be predicted. It is also clear that the predictably futile admissions involve patients who could be cared for more appropriately in less distressing settings.

We must develop admission criteria that more frequently restrict the use of intensive care to those patients who are likely to benefit from it. We need explicit criteria for excluding patients for whom no ultimate benefit can be predicted (in cases of brain death, rapidly progressing fatal illness, and the like), a larger proportion of patients for whom survival is extremely improbable (in cases involving failure of three or more vital organs), and patients for whom iatrogenic risks exceed the likelihood of potential benefits.

REFORMING CONSENT PROCEDURES

For historically complex reasons, intensive care units typically presume patients' consent to interventions. Many seek explicit consent only when contemplating a cessation of intervention—especially a cessation of life support.

This presumption is formalized in the do-not-resuscitate (DNR) protocols that developed during the 1970s which typically require explicit formal consent only for decisions not to intervene.[1] Thus, they presume that clinicians have the right to proceed with life-support intervention without the prior consent of the patient.

The problem of intervening without consent is compounded by three difficulties. The negative aura of DNR protocols leads clinicians to delay discussing the limitation of interventions with patients, effectively denying most patients the opportunity of directly participating even in the inverted consent process.[2] Decisionmaking thus tends to be shifted to families who, bereaved, are dismayed by the negative nature of the DNR decision and often ignorant of the patient's reflective desires and tend to be ambivalent about consenting to DNR orders. As a result, prognostically futile interventions con-

1. Critical Care Committee of the Massachusetts General Hospital, "Optimum Care for Hopelessly Ill Patients," and Mitchell T. Rabkin, Gerald Gillerman, and Nancy R. Rice, "Orders Not to Resuscitate," *New England Journal of Medicine*, vol. 295 (August 12, 1976), pp. 362–64 and 364–66.

2. Susanna E. Bedell and others, "Do-Not-Resuscitate Orders for Critically Ill Patients in the Hospital," *Journal of the American Medical Association*, vol. 25 (July 11, 1986), pp. 233–37; Susanna E. Bedell and Thomas L. Delbanco, "Choices about Cardiopulmonary Resuscitation in the Hospital: When Do Physicians Talk with Patients?" *New England Journal of Medicine*, vol. 310 (April 26, 1984), pp. 1089–93.

tinue, even though they are not recommended by clinicians, may not be positively desired by patients or families, deplete scarce intensive care resources, and may even deprive other patients of prognostically beneficial resources. A further irony, when cessation becomes hostage to familial uncertainty, is that some humanely motivated clinicians have reinstituted slow-codes and undocumented no-codes to resolve the problem.[3]

Consent is more than a signature on a paper that removes a legal constraint on the activities of clinicians; consent is the moral basis of contemporary medicine. Except in emergencies, interventions without consent, including cardiopulmonary resuscitation (CPR), are unacceptable. Therefore, DNR protocols should be replaced with procedures for obtaining positive consent for CPR and other standard intensive care interventions before patients are admitted to intensive care units. Once the medical community recognizes the need to replace DNR policies with a positive consent process, the practical problems confronting such a policy will be resolved.

It is not unreasonable to develop systematic procedures in which advance directives giving consent to resuscitate and to administer other intensive care interventions are requested of all preoperative surgery patients, all nursing home patients, and other likely candidates for intensive care technology. The advance directive process creates a natural context for asking patients to designate their own surrogates and to dictate a living will in which they direct clinicians not only to administer but also to limit intensive care interventions. Recent studies of the attitudes of patients at risk for intensive care interventions indicate that these patients are, in fact, willing to limit those interventions—but they do not communicate their views about the appropriate levels of intervention to their physicians.[4] A system of advance directives is likely to facilitate this communication and bring about a significant increase in the voluntary limitation of cardiopulmonary resuscitation and other intensive care interventions.

3. Robert Baker, "The Patient Who Wants to Fight," in Stanley Reiser and Michael Anbar, eds., *The Machine at the Bedside: Strategies for Using Medical Technology in Patient Care* (Cambridge University Press, 1984), pp. 213–20.

4. Bernard Lo, Gary A. McLeod, and Glenn Saika, "Patient Attitudes Discussing Life-Sustaining Treatment," *Archives of Internal Medicine*, vol. 146 (August 1986), pp. 1613–15.

ON LEADERSHIP AND THE LAW

Implementing our proposals requires significant modifications of current practices, not only in intensive care units, but in the general wards of hospitals and in nursing homes. It may also challenge some current interpretations of the law—although (we believe) it may not be thought of as conflicting with the letter or the spirit of any laws. The medical community has dealt with such complexities in the past. In 1968, for example, the Ad Hoc Committee of the Harvard Medical School to Examine the Definition of Brain Death published a statement calling on "responsible medical opinion" to "adopt new criteria for pronouncing death." The authors explained that, although the position that they were advocating required significant changes in medical practice and might conflict with then current interpretations of the law, "if this position is adopted by the medical community, it can form the basis for the current legal concept of death."[5] The committee was right; the medical community, acting through its professional organizations, was able to form a new societal consensus about the nature of death.

PROPOSAL TO MEDICAL SOCIETIES

We call on the American Medical Association, the American College of Physicians, the American College of Surgeons, the American Society of Anesthesiologists, the Society of Critical Care Medicine, and other professional medical organizations to endorse the concept of prognostic admissions policies, develop a consensus about the appropriateness of using prognostic estimates as part of a strategy to develop guidelines for admission to intensive care units, and support research projects designed to refine and develop the data required for prognostically based admissions standards. We recommend that inverted consent practices implicit in DNR policies be replaced by prior consent for cardiopulmonary resuscitation and other intensive care interventions, and that a model set of advance directives

5. Report of the Ad Hoc Committee of the Harved Medical School to Examine the Definition of Brain Death, "A Definition of Irreversible Coma," *Journal of the American Medical Association,* vol. 205 (August 5, 1968), p. 339.

be developed to implement a policy of positive consent to intensive care interventions.

The medical community is once again struggling with obsolete concepts of medical care—concepts that require the deployment of increasingly scarce resources on futile, expensive, and often inhumane intensive care interventions. We believe that the medical community, acting through its professional organizations, must again challenge administrative bodies, courts, and legislatures to rethink current standards for admission, treatment, and consent in intensive care units. We also believe that unless the medical community acts successfully, and quickly, to revise the practice of intensive care medicine, economic pressures will force the de facto rationing of intensive care resources, depriving some patients of effective, high-cost medical care.

Panel Participants

HENRY J. AARON, Senior Fellow, Economic Studies Program, Brookings Institution; Professor of Economics, University of Maryland; former Assistant Secretary for Planning and Evaluation, Department of Health, Education, and Welfare

JEFFREY S. AUGENSTEIN, Associate Professor of Surgery and Anesthesiology and Director of the Medical Computer Systems Laboratory, University of Miami School of Medicine

MARY ANN BAILY, Adjunct Associate Professor of Economics, George Washington University; Consultant, Office of Technology Assessment

ROBERT BAKER, Associate Professor of Philosophy and Director of the Computer in the Humanities Undergraduate Curriculum Program, Union College

HOWARD S. BERLINER, Associate Research Scientist, Conservation of Human Resources, Columbia University

JAMES D. CARROLL, Senior Staff Member, Center for Public Policy Education, Brookings Institution

I. ALAN FEIN, Assistant Professor of Medicine, Albany Medical College; Director of Surgical Critical Care and the Critical Care Medicine Fellowship, Ellis Hospital

J. RICHARD GAINTNER, President and Chief Executive Officer, Albany Medical Center

WILLIS D. GRADISON, JR., U.S. Representative, Second District of Ohio; ranking Republican member of the Health Subcommittee of the House Committee on Ways and Means

DENNIS M. GREENBAUM, Attending Physician, Department of Medicine, and Chief, Medical Intensive Care Unit, St. Vincent's Hospital and Medical Center of New York; President-elect of Society of Critical Care Medicine

BARBARA R. GRUMET, Assistant Professor, Department of Political Science and Public Administration, Russell Sage College; Adjunct Assistant Professor, Albany Medical College

WILLIAM A. KNAUS, Director of the Intensive Care Unit Research, George Washington University Medical Center

JAMES LAMBRINOS, Director of the Program in Health Systems Administration, Union College

JOHN S. MORRIS, President, Union College

MICHAEL A. RIE, Anesthesiologist and Internist, Respiratory Surgical Intensive Care Unit, Massachusetts General Hospital; Assistant Professor of Anesthesia, Harvard Medical School

LINDSAY ROBINSON, Vice President for Health Affairs, Albany Division, Empire Blue Cross and Blue Shield

MARTIN A. STROSBERG, Associate Professor, Program in Health Systems Administration, Union College

DANIEL TERES, Director, Adult Critical Care Services, Baystate Medical Center; Assistant Professor of Medicine and Associate Clinical Professor of Surgery, Tufts University School of Medicine; Associate Professor in Public Health, School of Public Health, University of Massachusetts

ROBERT M. VEATCH, Professor of Medical Ethics, Kennedy Institute of Ethics, Georgetown University

MAX HARRY WEIL, Professor and Chairman of Department of Medicine, University of Health Sciences, Chicago Medical School; Director, Annual Symposium on Critical Care Medicine, University of Southern California and Institute of Critical Care Medicine

Conference Participants

with their affiliations at the time of the conference

Richard G. Adams
Howard University Hospital

Rebecca Andrews
Medical College of Georgia

John Balint
Albany Medical College

Cheryl Bascomb
Union Mutual Life Insurance

Alfred D. Beasley
University of Tennessee Medical Hospital

Susan Beecher
Senate Special Committee on Aging

Clyde J. Behney
Office of Technology Assessment

Mark Benedict
House Subcommittee on Health and Long-Term Care

Marvin L. Birnbaum
University of Wisconsin Hospital

Michelle Black
George Washington University

Jody S. Bleier
Ellis Hospital

Joseph F. Boyle
American Society of Internal Medicine

Steven Boyle
Ellis Hospital

Robert Breault
Ellis Hospital

Mary C. Brecht
Office of Senator Dave Durenberger

Bonnie L. Brown
Office of Representative Willis D. Gradison, Jr.

Earl Canfield
Congressional Research Service

Betsy Carrier
American Postal Workers Union Health Plan

Samuel Ciccio
Albany Medical College

Cynthia B. Cohen
Hastings Center

Ian Cohen
Ellis Hospital

Ann Compson
Children's Hospital of Pittsburgh

Henry E. Damm
St. Clare's Hospital

Jeffrey B. Danilo
Health and Hospitals Corp.

Susan M. Dumsha
Union Memorial Hospital

Sandra Fein
Ellis Hospital

Florence Fiori
Department of Health and Human Services

Suzanne Fleming
Cooper Hospital

Andrew Gettinger
Dartmouth Medical School

Robert M. Giasi
University of Massachusetts Medical Center

John Gold
Ellis Hospital

Eugenia Hamilton
Mary Hitchcock Memorial Hospital

Joel Helfman
Ellis Hospital

Roger C. Herdman
Office of Technology Assessment

Melvin C. Hochman
Booth Memorial Medical Center

Mathilda Horst
Henry Ford Hospital

Michael S. Jastremski
Critical Care and Emergency Medical Services Group

Roslyn Jones
Ellis Hospital

Janet Kline
Congressional Research Service

Johnsey Leef, Jr.
Charleston Area Medical Center

Charles W. Lidz
University of Pittsburgh

Robert M. Liebers
Ellis Hospital

Diane Lifsey
Senate Special Committee on Aging

Stanley L. Loftness
Children's Hospital

Lawrence Maldonado
Cedars-Sinai Medical Center

William L. Marsh
George Washington University Hospital

Omar Mendez
Ellis Hospital

Kenneth Meyer
Ellis Hospital

Franklin Myers
Polyclinic Medical Center

Lucille Pippin
Emory University Hospital

Michael R. Pollard
Pharmaceuticals Manufacturers Association

William Power
Ellis Hospital

James A. Prevost
Joint Commission on Accreditation of Hospitals

Russell C. Raphaely
Children's Hospital of Philadelphia

Victor P. Raymond
House Veterans' Affairs Committee

Valerie Rinkle
Department of Health and Human Services

William H. Robinson
Congressional Research Service

Leonard Scherlis
House Subcommittee on Health and Long-Term Care

David W. Shively
Health Care Telecommunications Corp.

Suryanarayana Siram
Howard University Hospital

Charles Smith
Ellis Hospital

Joseph L. Smith
Geisinger Medical Center

James V. Snyder
Presbyterian-University Hospital

Charles L. Sprung
University of Miami School of Medicine

Joseph J. Stez
New England Medical Center

Anthony Tartaglia
Albany Medical Center

John P. Tooker
Maine Medical Center

Richard C. Treat
Medical College of Georgia

Carol J. Weil
American College of Physicians

Andrew Wood
Ellis Hospital

Thomas R. Wright
Hurley Medical Center

Joseph Zimmerman
Smith Kline & French Laboratories